Bread
of **Life**

Prayers for Eucharistic Adoration

Bread
of Life

Written and compiled by
Marie Paul Curley, FSP,
and Madonna Therese Ratliff, FSP

Pauline
BOOKS & MEDIA
Boston

Nihil Obstat: Rev. Brian E. Mahoney, S.T.L.

Imprimatur: ✠ Most Rev. Seán O'Malley, O.F.M. Cap.
Archbishop of Boston
September 2, 2004

Library of Congress Cataloging-in-Publication Data
Curley, Marie Paul.
  Bread of life : prayers for Eucharistic adoration / written
and compiled by Marie Paul Curley and Madonna Therese
Ratliff.
     p. cm.
  ISBN 0-8198-1167-X
  1. Lord's Supper—Adoration—Prayer-books and devo-
tions—English. I. Ratliff, Madonna Therese. II. Title.
  BX2233.C865 2004
  242'.802—dc22

                                               2004010724

Published by Pauline Books & Media, 50 Saint Pauls
Avenue, Boston, MA 02130-3491.

Printed in Korea

www.pauline.org

Pauline Books & Media is the publishing house of the
Daughters of St. Paul, an international congregation of
women religious serving the Church with the communica-
tions media.

1 2 3 4 5 6 7 8 9   11 10 09 08 07 06 05 04

Contents

Invitation

∽∼∾

Then he took bread, blessed it, broke it, and gave it to them saying, "This is my body which is given up for you—do this in my remembrance." Likewise he took the cup after he had eaten and said, "This cup is the new covenant in my blood which is poured out for you" (Luke 22:19–20*).

∽∼∾

The Eucharist is one of the most tangible ways God is present in our world today. If confusion or loneliness weighs too heavily on our hearts, if we struggle with meaninglessness, if we long to step off life's frantic treadmill and slow down to ponder the direction of our lives, Jesus invites us, "Come to me." The Eucharist can become our safest refuge where we share with Jesus our vulnerability, our pain, our weakness, and where we bring our concerns for others, our worries for the wounds of the world, hoping to find them transformed into his joy, his love, and his peace.

At every Mass, or Eucharistic Celebration, we can discover anew how much our Triune God loves us. The Father sends his Beloved Son who shares our common humanity, walks with us, and shows us the way to the deepest possible fulfillment, and then gives himself completely to us, pouring out for love of us his very life in his passion, death, and resurrection, leaving with us the indwelling Spirit. It is Jesus' loving gift of his life, offering himself to the Father, that we participate in at every Eucharist: "This is my Body and Blood, given for you."

The Eucharist is God's greatest gift to us—it is where Jesus' heart meets the needs of the world on a daily basis. If we want to fully, faithfully live our Christian vocation, we need to be rooted in the Eucharist.

We center our lives in the Eucharist by giving priority to the Celebration of the Eucharist: attentively listening to the proclaimed Word of God, truly uniting ourselves with Je-

sus in his offering to the Father, joyfully receiving the loving embrace of Jesus in Communion, and going forth as the Body of
Christ, renewed in our determination to love
and to serve. Thus, the Sunday Eucharist becomes the center of our week; if we are able
to attend daily Mass, it becomes the focal
point of our day. Eucharistic adoration, or
prayer before Jesus in the Blessed Sacrament,
becomes a way to enrich our participation in
the Eucharistic Celebration. Adoring Jesus in
this way allows us personal time to more
deeply immerse ourselves in the Paschal Mystery so that we begin to take on Jesus' own attitudes, way of life, and love for the Father.

Eucharistic adoration can be a powerfully
transforming experience. The deeper our Eucharistic prayer, the more fully we are able to
participate in the Eucharistic Celebration and
the more fully we are transformed in Christ—
both in the liturgy we celebrate together and
in our daily lives. This prayer book, drawn
from Scripture, the saints, the wisdom of the
Church, contemporary spiritual writers, and
the needs of pray-ers today, offers a compre-
hensive resource for those who would like to

enrich their Eucharistic prayer, as well as for those who would like to begin but aren't sure where to start. Each section of the prayer book is designed for a particular way of praying or for a particular moment that naturally arises out of time spent in adoration.

———— · ————

Prayer-Starters

The prayer book begins with *Prayer-Starters*, intended for when we have just a few moments to pray before Jesus in the Eucharist, or for those times when we just can't seem to focus in prayer—when we are distracted, or perhaps anxious, or bored. Each "prayer-starter" entices us to enter into an encounter with Jesus.

———— · ————

Listening to Love
Eucharistic Readings

This section offers a series of reflections that are meant to help deepen our understanding of and appreciation for the Eucharistic Mystery. These readings can be used for meditation or to "set the tone" for a longer time of prayer, such as an hour of adoration. The key to meditation or spiritual reading is to reflect on the reading and apply it to our own lives, following up our reflection with an act of faith or personal commitment to the Lord.

Prayers

The center of the prayer book is found in the next seven sections, which focus on the classic purposes of prayer: adoration, praise, sorrow, and intercession. All of these prayers can be used freely during times of adoration:

- *Kneeling Before Our God: Prayers of Adoration;*
- *Delighting in His Presence: Prayers of Praise and Thanksgiving;*
- *Encountering Merciful Love: Prayers for Conversion and Healing...*

The prayers of intercession are broken into three sections to make it easier to find prayers for various needs:

- *Drawing Near in Confidence: Petitions and Prayers for Personal Transformation* focuses on prayers for personal growth and holiness.
- *Nourishing Our Lives: Prayers from the Hearts of Believers* provides a selection of prayers for needs experienced in everyday life.
- *Interceding for the World: Prayers for Particular Needs* helps us to bring to the Lord the dreams and darkness of humanity, asking that they be transformed into a longing for the full coming of the Kingdom of God.

A selection of *Favorite Eucharistic Hymns* provides a resource for those who participate in group adoration together.

———

Adoring Jesus Way, Truth, and Life
Hours of Adoration

The last section explains how to make an hour of adoration in the Eucharistic presence of Jesus, highlighting the Pauline method of bringing to Jesus all that we are, to be transformed in him. This section includes three complete hours of adoration, as well as suggested Scripture readings for additional hours of adoration on various themes. If you find this section is helpful, you may wish to read a more complete explanation of the Pauline hour of adoration, found in the book *Life for the World,* which includes an additional twelve hours of adoration for personal or group use.

———

The Eucharist is an unfathomable gift of divine love. When we consistently spend time with Jesus in the Eucharist, we discover that our ways of thinking, acting, and loving gradually become more and more Christ-like. We glimpse Jesus' own relationship with the Father and the Spirit—and we begin to enter into the inner life of the Trinity, embraced in their eternal communion of Love. Having discovered that in Christ we are God's beloved, we begin to fully live out our call to bring our world into deeper communion with Jesus and, in him, with the Father and the Spirit.

Prayer~Starters

∽∾∽

A morsel of bread is more real
than the universe, more full of
existence, more full of the
Word—a song overflowing
the sea, a mist confusing the
sundial—God in exile.

—*Karol Wojtyla*

"Come to me, all you grown weary and
  burdened,
and I will refresh you.
Take my yoke upon you
and learn from me,
for I am gentle and humble hearted,
and you will find rest for your souls;
For my yoke is easy,
and my burden light."
  —Jesus (Mt 11:28–30*)

——— • ———

I adore you, most sacred Eucharistic Heart of
Jesus!
  —Traditional

——— • ———

The time we spend in having our daily audience with God is the most precious part of
the whole day.
  —Blessed Teresa of Calcutta

——— • ———

Hovering over creation, the Holy Spirit made the universe. Hovering over the Virgin Mary, the Spirit gave flesh to the Word. This same Spirit, hovering over bread and wine, transforms them into the sacramental Body and Blood of Christ. And this Spirit hovers over me!

—Lawrence E. Corcoran, SJ

———

For me, prayer is an aspiration of the heart, it is a simple glance directed to heaven, it is a cry of gratitude and love in the midst of trial as well as joy; finally, it is something great, supernatural, which expands my soul and unites me to Jesus.

—Saint Thérèse of Lisieux

———

An Hour of Adoration prepares one for the celebration and reception of the Holy Eucharist. Frequent encounters and familiar conversation with Jesus produce friendship, resemblance, and identity of thought, feeling, and willing with Jesus.

—Blessed James Alberione

———

Pause before the tabernacle by yourself, for no special reason, even without saying a word, simply remaining in Christ's presence, contemplating the supreme gesture of love contained in the consecrated Bread.

—Pope John Paul II

If we really love the good God, we will find it a joy and happiness to spend some time near him, to adore him, and keep company with so good a friend. He is there in the tabernacle. What is Jesus doing in this sacrament of love? He is loving us.

—Saint John Vianney

Communion means living in Christ and letting Christ live in me, as the Apostle Paul expressed so powerfully (cf. Rom 6:10; Gal 2:20); to become, like him and in him, effective instruments in the loving plan of the Blessed Trinity, who through the Church wants to make one family of all people.

—Pope John Paul II

I put before you
the one great thing
to love on earth:
the Blessed Sacrament.
There you will find romance,
glory, honor, fidelity,
and the true way
of all your loves on earth
and more than that.

—J. R. R. Tolkien

Abide in me as I abide in you. Just as the
branch cannot bear fruit by itself unless it
abides in the vine, neither can you unless you
abide in me. I am the vine, you are the
branches. Those who abide in me and I in
them bear much fruit, because apart from me
you can do nothing.... If you abide in me,
and my words abide in you, ask for whatever
you wish, and it will be done for you.

—Jesus (Jn 15:4–7)

Your face, LORD, do I seek.

—Psalm 27

The time we spend in having our daily audience with God is the most precious part of the whole day.

—Blessed Teresa of Calcutta

——— —

"Lord, to whom can we go? You have the words of eternal life. We have come to believe and know that you are the Holy One of God."

—Saint Peter (Jn 6:68–69)

——— —

We cannot love God unless we love each other, and to love we must know each other. We know him in the breaking of bread, and we are not alone anymore. Heaven is a banquet and life is a banquet, too, even with a crust, where there is companionship.

We have all known the long loneliness and we have learned that the only solution is love and that love comes with community.

—Dorothy Day

——— —

When a soul holds onto trust in God—
whether in searching or in contemplation—
this is the highest worship she can bring.
    —Blessed Julian of Norwich

With so much of the world living in hunger,
how could God *not* but come as Bread?
    —Attributed to Gandhi, commenting on the Chris-
    tian belief in the Eucharist

Bread-breakers become bread broken; the
diners become the world's dinner; the body
at the table becomes the body *on* the table.
For the life of the world.
    —Nathan Mitchell

Jesus transforms a white particle into himself
every day in order to communicate his life to
you. What's more, with a love that is greater
still, he wants to transform you into himself.
    —Saint Thérèse of Lisieux

The thirst for God cannot be uprooted from the human heart. Some questions find an answer only in personal contact with Christ. Only in intimacy with him does every existence acquire meaning and succeed in experiencing joy.

—Pope John Paul II

He was wounded for our transgressions, crushed for our iniquities; upon him was the punishment that made us whole, and by his bruises we are healed.

—Isaiah 53:5

Sing to the LORD a new song!

—Psalm 149

Prayer is a meeting which nourishes our hearts. It is presence and communion. The secret of our being is in this kiss of God by which we know we are loved and forgiven.

—Jean Vanier

Jesus is present and lives in our midst in the Eucharist. Let us listen to him for he is truth. Let us look at him, for he is the face of the Father. Let us love him, for he is love giving himself to his creatures. He comes to our soul so that it may disappear in him and become divine. What union, however great, can compare to this?

—Saint Teresa de Los Andes

Lord, teach me to pray.

—A disciple of Jesus (cf. Lk 11:1)

I turn most truly for solace, for strength to endure, to the psalms. I may read them without understanding, and mechanically at first, but I do believe they are the Word, and that Scripture on the one hand and the Eucharist, the Word made Flesh, on the other, have in them that strength which no power on earth can withstand.

—Dorothy Day

Christ will not deceive us. That is why our lives must be woven around the Eucharist. The Christ who gives of himself to us under the appearance of bread and the Christ who is hidden under the distressing disguise of the poor is the same Jesus.

—Blessed Teresa of Calcutta

"I am the Bread of Life."

—Jesus (Jn 6:48)

Neither death, nor life, nor angels, nor rulers, nor things present, nor things to come, nor powers, nor height, nor depth, nor anything else in all creation, will be able to separate us from the love of God in Christ Jesus our Lord.

—Saint Paul (Rom 8:38–39)

My God, take my heart.
Set it on fire!

—Saint Bernadette Soubirous

To make room in our life for the Eucharistic
Lord, so that he can change our life into
his—is that asking too much?
  —Saint Edith Stein

——— — ———

A true Eucharist is never a passive, comforting moment alone with God, something
which allows us to escape the cares and concerns of our everyday life. Eucharist is where
all these cares and concerns come to a focus,
and where we are asked to measure them
against the standard lived by Jesus when he
proclaimed for all to hear that the bread that
he would give would provide life for the entire world. But it will do so only if, finding
ourselves with a basket of bread, we have
peered deeply enough into the heart of
Christ to know what to do with it.
  —Paul Bernier

——— — ———

"Father, into your hands I commend my
spirit."
  —Jesus (Lk 23:46)

——— — ———

The Mass is not just a way of worshiping, but a way of living.

—William Ogrodowski

We come to the Eucharist with hearts broken by many losses, our own as well as those of the world.... The great mystery we celebrate in the Eucharist and live in a Eucharistic life is precisely that through mourning our losses we come to know life as a gift.

—Henri J. M. Nouwen

Give thanks to the LORD, for he is good, for his love is everlasting!

—Psalm 136:1

Receiving Communion is not like picturing with the imagination, as when we reflect up-on the Lord on the cross or in other episodes of the passion.... In Communion the event is happening now, and it is entirely true.

—Saint Teresa of Avila

Jesus wants to possess your heart completely.
  He wants you to be a great saint.
The good God never asks the impossible.
  —Saint Thérèse of Lisieux

——— ———

When we are shaken by the sight of evil
spreading in the universe...we should not
forget that such unleashing of the forces of
sin is overcome by the saving power of
Christ. Whenever the words of consecration
are uttered in the Mass and the Body and
Blood of Christ become present in the act of
the sacrifice, the triumph of love over hatred,
of holiness over sin, is also present. Every
Eucharistic Celebration is stronger than all
the evil in the universe; it means real, concrete accomplishment of the redemption.
  —Pope John Paul II

——— ———

So now in the sacrament of Eucharistic love
he still abides in littleness to stay with us always.
  —Saint Katharine Drexel

——— ———

"Could you not stay awake with me one
hour?"
    —Jesus (Mt 26:40)

——— • ———

I follow Christ:
Jesus is my God,
Jesus is my Spouse,
Jesus is my life,
Jesus is my only love,
Jesus is my all in all;
Jesus is my everything.
    —Blessed Teresa of Calcutta

——— • ———

The LORD is my chosen portion and my cup.
    —Psalm 16:5

——— • ———

You will learn to integrate yourself, pull
yourself together, in the way we are speaking
of, precisely in proportion as you manage to
get more closely in touch, and more intimately in touch, with the Eucharistic life of our
blessed Lord. The Blessed Sacrament is the
Sacrament of Unity; and when you receive it,

it does not merely produce in you more char~
ity toward your neighbor, more loyalty
toward the Church, more unselfishness in
your human attachments. It makes you more
at unity with yourself; it catches up your life
into a rhythm that echoes the heavenly mu~
sic.... It comes to you...full of that unifying
love which is the bond of the Blessed Trinity.

—Ronald Knox

Realize that you may gain more in a quarter
of an hour of prayer before the Blessed
Sacrament than in all the other spiritual
practices of the day.

—Saint Alphonsus Liguori

My Lord, I am entirely the work of your all~
powerful love. I adore you, my God, one in
nature and triune in Persons. I thank you,
because you have made me for the happiness
which lies in you and for your eternal glory.
Save me with your love and your mercy!

—Blessed James Alberione

I am God's wheat, ground fine by the lion's teeth to be made purest bread for Christ.

—Saint Ignatius of Antioch

———

Rejoice in the Lord always; again I will say, Rejoice. Let your gentleness be known to everyone. The Lord is near.

—Saint Paul (Phil 4:4–5)

———

Be my life, my love, my all!

—Saint Margaret Mary Alacoque

———

Listen in silence because if your heart is full of other things, you cannot hear the voice of God.... The essential thing is not what we say, but what God says to us and through us.

—Blessed Teresa of Calcutta

———

I am the way, the truth, and the life.

—Jesus (Jn 14:6)

Listening to Love
Eucharistic Readings

❧❧❧

Our present time and the future of the world are illuminated by Christ's Eucharistic presence and are desperate for his action.

—*Blessed James Alberione*

I Am the Bread of Life
John 6:32–40

Jesus said to them, "Very truly, I tell you, it was not Moses who gave you the bread from heaven, but it is my Father who gives you the true bread from heaven. For the bread of God is that which comes down from heaven and gives life to the world."

They said to him, "Sir, give us this bread always." Jesus said to them, "I am the Bread of Life. Whoever comes to me will never be hungry, and whoever believes in me will never be thirsty. But I said to you that you have seen me and yet do not believe.

"Everything that the Father gives me will come to me, and anyone who comes to me I will never drive away; for I have come down from heaven, not to do my own will, but the will of him who sent me. And this is the will of him who sent me, that I should lose nothing of all that he has given me, but raise it up on the last day."

———— • ————

Becoming the Kernels of Wheat
By Ronald Rolheiser, OMI

When we ritually tell the story of Jesus' sacrifice (in the Eucharistic prayer, the very heart of liturgy), we experience the "real presence" of the event of Christ's dying and rising, and we participate in it. How? We participate in Jesus' sacrifice for us when we, like him, let ourselves be broken down, when we, like him, become selfless. The Eucharist, as sacrifice, invites us to become like the kernels of wheat that make up the bread and the clusters of grapes that make up the wine, broken down and crushed so that we can become part of communal loaf and single cup.

Occasionally when Saint Augustine was giving the Eucharist to a communicant, instead of saying, "The body of Christ," he would say: "Receive what you are." That puts things correctly. What is supposed to happen at the Eucharist is that we, the congregation, by sacrificing the things that divide us, should become the Body and Blood of Christ.

More so than the bread and wine, we, the people, are meant to be changed, to be transubstantiated. The Eucharist, as sacrifice, asks us to become the bread of brokenness and the chalice of vulnerability.

———

Opening My Heart to Everyone
By Catherine de Hueck Doherty

Looking out of the window...I suddenly saw how tenderly, how gently, how warmly, how lovingly Christ bends toward the world. At that moment I also understood the words "cosmic charity," and when these words touched me, they expanded my heart to embrace especially all those who are weak and who keep on falling.

But then I looked again and I realized that everyone is weak and everyone falls! Does that mean that to be pure of heart one must love everyone? Yes...I have to open my heart to everyone who is weak, and that means *everyone*. Now I know why the pure of heart shall see God, and even see him now, *because he is in the ones who are weak.*

Yes, he will be in them, in each one of them, and that thought brought me to...the Eucharist. I saw the bread given to everyone present and I realized vividly and clearly that everyone among those present, including myself, was weak, prone to failing and falling again and again, and somehow I understood with the heart what the beatitude meant.

———

What Is the Meaning of Life?
By Massino Camisasca

What, in their deepest meaning, are the years of our life about? They are about the adventure of knowing Christ, the adventure of experiencing Christ and ourselves, which is the best and greatest adventure.

The liturgy *is* Christ making himself known to us day by day. Day by day, the Eucharistic Celebration and the Liturgy of the Hours make Scripture present. Each word they contain is a ray of Christ's beauty, a particle of his life, of the mystery of his person.

Day by day, the Mass and Eucharistic adoration place us before the unfathomable abyss of the Incarnation. The Eucharist is itself the extreme, crazy, impossible consequence of the Incarnation. Identification with Christ in meditation on Scripture and participation in the Eucharist will never open up for us unless it is born from the desire to see him who loves us and whom we love.

Love One Another As I Have Loved You
By Blessed Teresa of Calcutta

Jesus says time and again that we have to love one another. He had to come for that purpose: to tell us that God loves us, that we are precious to him, that we have been created to love and to be loved, and that we must love one another as he loves us, as the Father has loved him.... When we look at the cross we know how he loved us. And when we look at the tabernacle, we know how he loves us still. That is why he made himself the Bread of Life: we just forget this tenderness of love.

And he made himself this Bread of Life to satisfy our hunger for his love. And as if that were not enough for him, he made himself the hungry one, the naked one, the humblest one so that you and I can satisfy his hunger for our human love. This is something so wonderful— the sick, the poor, the unwanted, the unloved—Christ in his distressing disguises....

Sacrifice is necessary in our lives if we want to realize the tenderness of God's love. Sacrifice is his love in action. God sent Jesus to teach us this love...I beg you to get closer to the Eucharist and to Jesus.... We must pray to Jesus to give us that tenderness of the Eucharist.

Eucharist, the Center of Catholic Prayer
By Cardinal Roger Mahony

After the Prayer over the Gifts, the Eucharistic Prayer begins. Here we are at the center of Catholic praying and that center is Eucharistic.... Great mystery is conveyed in the faces and postures, singing and silence, gesture and word. Everyone is attentive, bodies engaged as much as their hearts. It is clearly the central moment of this Lord's Day gathering.

Over the altar and the gifts of bread and wine, all God's saving deeds are remembered, all is held up in praise of God, all is asked of God. The Catholic sensibility to sacrament, to the presence of God, is never more joyous, never more challenging.

We need to take care in our thinking and in our language: When we say "Eucharist," we mean this whole action of presider and assembly. That is the Eucharist whose grace and powerful mystery can transform us and, in us, the world.... Nothing more clearly and wonderfully defines who we are as Catholics as does the celebration of the Eucharist, the Sacrifice of the Mass.

The Paschal Banquet
By Pope John Paul II

In instituting the Eucharist, Jesus did not merely say: "This is my body," "this is my blood," but went on to add: "which is given for you," "which is poured out for you" (Lk 22:19–20). Jesus did not simply state that what he was giving them to eat and drink was his Body and his Blood; he also expressed *its sacrificial meaning* and made sacramentally present his sacrifice which would soon be offered on the cross for the salvation of all.

The Church constantly draws her life from this redeeming sacrifice; she approaches it not only through faith-filled remembrance, but also through a real contact, since *this sacrifice is made present ever anew,* sacramentally perpetuated, in every community which offers it. The Eucharist thus applies to men and women today the reconciliation won once for all by Christ for mankind in every age.

The Lord wished to remain with us in the Eucharist, making his presence in meal and sacrifice the promise of a humanity renewed by his love.... Proclaiming the death of the Lord "until he comes" (1 Cor 11:26) entails that all who take part in the Eucharist be committed to changing their lives and making them in a certain way completely "Eucharistic."

Our Self~Giving God

By Henri J. M. Nouwen

Jesus is God~for~us, God~with~us, God~within~us. Jesus is God giving himself completely, pouring himself out for us without reserve.

In the Eucharist, Jesus gives all. The bread is not simply a sign of his desire to become our food; the cup is not just a sign of his willingness to be our drink. Bread and wine *become* his Body and Blood in the giving.... God does not hold back; God gives all.

Incarnation and Eucharist are the two expressions of the immense, self~giving love of God. And so the sacrifice on the cross and the sacrifice at the table are one sacrifice, one complete, divine self~giving that reaches out to all humanity in time and space.

Communion with Jesus means becoming like him. Communion, becoming Christ, leads us to a new realm of being. There we belong to Christ and Christ to us, and with Christ we belong to God.

Our participation in the inner life of God leads us to a new way of participation in each other's lives.... This new body is a spiritual body, fashioned by the Spirit of love. It manifests itself in very concrete ways: in forgiveness, reconciliation, mutual support, outreach to people in need, solidarity with all who suffer, and an ever-increasing concern for justice and peace. Thus communion not only creates community, but community always leads to mission.

———— ‑ ————

Renewing Our Faith
By Caroll Stuhlmueller

The Eucharist prepares us to return to daily life with a more sensitive awareness of Jesus' presence. By profound experience of God at prayer and the reading of Scripture, we become all the more conscious of Jesus' otherwise hidden presence in all the other moments of life. With renewed faith, we ought to be able to look hopefully and enthusiastically at life all about us.

Some important questions come to mind. Do we believe that Jesus can take our most crippled moments and transform them into great possibilities? Do we believe that Jesus can work miracles today? Are we able to slough off discouragement and frustration, and vigorously turn ourselves around and return to the holy city of divine accomplishments?

———— ——

You Become the Body of Christ
By Saint Augustine of Hippo

By bread, you are instructed as to how you ought to cherish unity. Was that bread made of one grain of wheat? Were there not, rather, many grains? However, before they became bread, these grains were separate; they were joined together in water after a certain amount of crushing. For, unless the grain is ground and moistened with water, it cannot arrive at that form which is called bread.

So, too, you were previously ground, as it were, by the humiliation of your fasting and by the sacrament of exorcism. Then came the Baptism of water; you were moistened, as it were, so to arrive at the form of bread. But without fire, bread does not exist. What, then, does fire signify? The chrism. For the sacrament of the Holy Spirit is the oil of our fire.... Therefore, the fire, that is, the Holy Spirit, comes after the water, then you become bread, that is, the body of Christ.

———— - ————

Jesus, God's Hospitality
By Monika Hellwig

Because Eucharist is first and foremost the celebration of divine hospitality made present to us in the person of Jesus, it is an action which addresses every form of inhospitality in our world, confronting it with the image of what might be and ought to be.

Jesus as the outreach of divine hospitality is not only the primary hospitality of all creation but the further redemptive hospitality of healing grace. At its simplest level of sharing of food, the Eucharist signals that in God's world, there is room for all. We are therefore challenged to solve the problems of the world by sharing, not by eliminating people, not by killing.

At its higher level of symbolism, pointing to the paschal mystery as foreshadowed by the Exodus event, the Eucharist bids us share in celebrating the liberation of the poor, the oppressed and the marginalized or excluded because these are in a special way the people of God.

———— —

Eucharist: the Sacrament of Life
By Pierre Teilhard de Chardin, SJ

The total offer that is made to me, I can only answer by a total acceptance. I shall therefore react to the Eucharistic contact with *the entire effort of my life*—of my life of to-day and my life of tomorrow, of my personal life and of my life as linked to all other lives.

Periodically, the sacred species may per-haps fade away in me. But each time they will leave me a little more deeply engulfed in the layers of your omnipotence: Living and dying, I shall never at any moment cease to move forward in you. Thus, the precept implicit in your Church, that we must communicate everywhere and always, is justified with ex-traordinary force and precision.

The Eucharist must invade my life. My life must become, as a result of the sacrament, an unlimited and endless contact with you—that life, which seemed a few moments ago, like a Baptism with you in the waters of the world, now reveals itself to me as communion with you through the world.

It is the sacrament of life. *The sacrament of my life*—of my life received, of my life lived, of my life surrendered.

Liturgy: The Path to Our Neighbor
By Cardinal Richard Cushing

How can we continually receive the Eucharistic Christ and leave untouched or unchanged any bitter or hardened prejudice against any member of any race of people? We tell ourselves that we mean no harm to anyone. Yet at the same time, we repeat the cheap racial joke, we make the ill-advised remark, we indulge in self-righteous anger in the home—all these plant the seed of a whole new generation of prejudice in our children. It seems so unimportant, so trivial. But multiply it by thousands and it becomes a cancer of sinful attitudes which sickens and weakens the body of the Church. Small wonder that we ask how can it be the same Christ that we love....

Liturgy, understood as the worship of the Church...and social action, understood as the work of the Church...are part, one of the other. Liturgy that does not move its participants to social action is mere ceremonialism; social action that does not find its source in the liturgy is mere humanitarianism.

I Am the Living Bread
John 6:47–57

"Very truly, I tell you, whoever believes has eternal life. I am the Bread of Life. Your ancestors ate the manna in the wilderness, and they died. This is the bread that comes down from heaven, so that one may eat of it and not die.

"I am the living bread that came down from heaven. Whoever eats of this bread will live forever; and the bread that I will give for the life of the world is my flesh." The Jews then disputed among themselves, saying, "How can this man give us his flesh to eat?"

So Jesus said to them, "Very truly, I tell you, unless you eat the flesh of the Son of Man and drink his blood, you have no life in you. Those who eat my flesh and drink my blood have eternal life, and I will raise them up on the last day; for my flesh is true food and my blood is true drink. Those who eat my flesh and drink my blood abide in me, and I in them.

"Just as the living Father sent me, and I live because of the Father, so whoever eats me will live because of me."

The Host Life
By Caryll Houselander

Living the Christ-life means that we are given the power of Christ's love…. It is almost frightening to seek an answer to the question: "Why does God remain in our midst silent and passive, knowing and seeing everything, but saying and doing nothing, while cruelty, injustice, ignorance, and misery go on and on and on?"

It is a frightening question until we remember what it is which alone *can* restore humanity to happiness: namely, supernatural life, beginning secretly in each individual heart; just as Incarnate Love began secretly on earth in the heart of Mary. It is one thing only, the birth of the infant Christ in us, Incarnate Love.

No voice of warning could effect this. That could make people tremble; it could not make them love. No armed force could do it, not even supernatural force. That could make people slaves; love is always free.

Love must begin from within. It must be sown in the inmost darkness of the human heart....

In the host, Christ gives himself to live the ordinary life as it is today...to take into himself the most ordinary, the most numerous, seemingly the most mediocre lives, bestowing upon them his own power to bring down the Spirit of Love. In those who have received him in Holy Communion, Christ goes among whom he will, to whatever places he chooses to be in.

Washing Each Others' Feet
By Ronald Rolheiser, OMI

We should be on our knees washing each others' feet because that is precisely what Jesus did at the first Eucharist, teaching us that the Eucharist is not a private act of devotion, meant to square our debts with God, but a call *to* and a grace *for* service. The Eucharist sends us out into the world ready to give expression to Christ's hospitality, humility, and self-effacement.

Where do we get such a notion? It lies at the very heart of the Eucharist itself. Jesus tells us this when he gives us the Eucharist, with the words: "Receive, give thanks, break, and share." The Eucharist invites us to receive nourishment from God, to be filled with gratitude, and, on the basis of that, to break open our lives and serve the poor in hospitality, humility, and self-donation.

It is no accident that, among all the potential Scripture texts it might have picked for liturgy on Holy Thursday, the Church has chosen to use John's account of Jesus washing the feet of disciples. A splendid choice. Indeed, nothing better expresses the meaning of the Eucharist than does that gesture.

Adoring in the Silence
By Thomas Merton

Active participation in the Mass, intelligent and humble reception of the Blessed Sacrament with a pure heart and the desire of perfect charity—these are the great remedies for the resentment and disunity that are spread by materialism. Here in this greatest of sacraments we can find the medicine that will purify our hearts from the contagion which they inevitably contract in a world that does not know God.

But in order to protect ourselves still more, to strengthen our position and to sink our roots deeper into the charity of Christ, it is necessary that we seek opportunities to adore Christ in this Blessed Sacrament and to give testimony to our faith outside the time of Mass. Therefore we visit our churches in order to pray to him in silence and alone.

We Remember the Bread of Life
By Joyce Rupp

Jesus, we remember who you are as the
   bread of our lives:
You are the One who enters into the hungry
   places of our hearts, wanting to convince
   us of your deep, abiding love.
You are the One who invites us constantly to
   choose life, even when our world, and
   sometimes our own inner places, taste of
   death, pain, and weariness.
You are the One who becomes our spiritual
   energy, inviting us to yearn for truth and
   to grow from its treasures.

We remember how you gift us with this
   bread:
This bread is strength for us when times are
   tough.

This bread must be broken before it can be
shared.

This bread, when taken within, transforms
the quality of our presence.

This bread, which houses the sacred in common earthen gifts, proclaims that the ordinary is but a mask of the holy.

We remember what this bread asks of us:

To be patient with our own growth, to recognize the process of our journey, to yield
to the nourishment which is waiting for us
if we will but come to the table.

To be your leaven so that faith can rise in the
hearts of others.

To be so deeply welded to compassion that
our hearts always save a space for the tears
of the world.

Eucharist: The Path to Unity
By Cardinal Joseph Bernardin

To give ourselves fully to the sojourning
dimension of our lives, knowing that the
manna of our God is blessing enough for our
need as we yearn for our true home.

The commitment I envision must be in our Catholic bones: the need to assemble each Sunday, to make common prayer in song, to hear Scriptures and reflect on them, to intercede for all the world, to gather at the holy table and give God thanks and praise over the bread and wine which are for us the Body and Blood of our Lord Jesus Christ, and finally to go from that room to our separate worlds—but now carrying the tune we have heard, murmuring the words we have made ours, nourished by the sacred banquet....

At this table we put aside every worldly separation based on culture, class, or other differences. This communion is why all prejudice, all racism, all sexism, all deference to wealth and power must be banished from our parishes, our homes, and our lives. This communion is why we will not call enemies those who are human beings like ourselves. This communion is why we will not commit the world's resources to an escalating arms race while the poor die. We cannot. Not when we have feasted here on the "body broken" and "blood poured out" for the life of the world.

A Posture of Worship
By Saint Cyril of Jerusalem

Coming up to receive, therefore, do not approach with your wrists extended or your fingers splayed, but making your left hand a throne for the right (for it is about to receive a King) and cupping your palm, so receive the Body of Christ; and answer "Amen." Carefully hallow your eyes by the touch of the sacred body, and then partake, taking care to lose no part of it. Such a loss would be like a mutilation of your own body. Why if you had been given gold-dust, would you not take the utmost care to hold it fast, not letting a grain slip through your fingers, lest you be by so much the poorer? How much more carefully, then, will you guard against losing so much as a crumb of that which is more precious than gold or precious stones!

After partaking of the Body of Christ, approach also the chalice of his Blood. Do not stretch out your hands, but, bowing low in a posture of worship and reverence as you say, "Amen," sanctify yourself by receiving also the Blood of Christ.

On the Day Called Sunday
By Saint Justin

Those who have more come to the aid of those who lack, and we are constantly together. Over all that we receive we bless the Maker of all things through his Son Jesus Christ and through the Holy Spirit. And on the day called Sunday there is a meeting in one place of those who live in cities or the country, and the memoirs of the apostles or the writings of the prophets are read as long as time permits. Then we all stand up together and offer prayers. And, as said before, when we have finished the prayer, bread is brought, and wine and water, and the president similarly sends up prayers and thanksgivings to the best of his ability, and the congregation assents, saying the Amen; the distribution and reception of the consecrated [elements] by each one takes place and they are sent to the absent by the deacons. Those who prosper, and who so wish, contribute, each one as much as each chooses to. What is collected is deposited with the president, and he takes care of orphans and widows, and those who are in want.

We, Too, Must Offer Our Bodies
By Archbishop Oscar Romero

We have just heard in the Gospel that those who surrender to the service of people through love of Christ will live like the grain of wheat that dies. This hope comforts us as Christians. We know that every effort to improve society, above all when society is so full of injustice and sin, is an effort that God blesses, wants, and demands. We have the security of knowing that what we plant, if nourished with Christian hope, will never fail.

This holy Mass, this Eucharist, is clearly an act of faith. This body broken and blood shed for human beings encourages us to give our body and blood up to suffering and pain, as Christ did—not for self, but to bring justice and peace to our people. Let us be intimately united in faith and hope at this moment.

At this point, Archbishop Romero was shot to death.

——— ———

Mary: Woman of the Eucharist
By Pope John Paul II

When, at the Visitation, Mary bore in her womb the Word made flesh, she became in some way a "tabernacle"—the first "tabernacle" in history—in which the Son of God, still invisible to our human gaze, allowed himself to be adored by Elizabeth, radiating his light as it were through the eyes and the voice of Mary. And is not the enraptured gaze of Mary as she contemplated the face of the newborn Christ and cradled him in her arms that unparalleled model of love which should inspire us every time we receive Eucharistic communion?

Mary, at the side of Christ throughout her life, made her own the sacrificial dimension of the Eucharist. The *Magnificat* expresses Mary's spirituality, and there is nothing greater than this spirituality for helping us to experience the mystery of the Eucharist. The Eucharist has been given to us so that our life, like that of Mary, may become completely a *Magnificat!*

Eucharistic Healing

By Matthew Linn, SJ, and Dennis Linn

"Go in peace to love and serve the Lord" has replaced the ending, "Go, the Mass is ended," because the Mass and its healing continues as we bring Christ into our homes and community. Healing happens not just around an altar but in a community whenever people meet Christ's love in each other.... We need help in laying down our lives as totally as Jesus did on the cross and continues to do in the Eucharist. For instance, if a family came to us without food, clothing, or education, and needed a home, health care, and a job, could we meet all their needs? No matter what a person needs, we need a community because none of us alone has all the resources to care for someone as lovingly as Christ cares. As we in a loving community take care of each other's needs, we begin to heal our painful memories and live out the Eucharist.

Everything Yearns for God
By Carlo Carretto

No, the Eucharist is not something strange: it is the most logical thing in the world, it is the story of the greatest love ever lived in this world, by a man called Jesus.

When I gaze on this bread, when I take this bread into my hands, I gaze on and take up the passion and death of Christ for humanity. This bread is the memorial of his death for us. This bread is the trumpet call of the resurrection, through which we, too, shall one day be able to rise.

This bread is the living summary of all God's love for man. From Genesis to the prophets, from Exodus to the Apocalypse, everything is yearning toward this terrible mystery of God's tragic love for man. God who made himself present in the first covenant yet more present in the Incarnation, becomes still more present in this mystery of the Bread of Life.

An Extraordinary Incarnation
By Louise Perrotta

Every time we go to Mass, we hear the familiar words, "This is my body... This is my blood..." Do we ever find them odd? Do we ever ask what it means, really, to eat the Body and Blood of Christ?

Right from the early days of the Church, the very idea of eating Christ's Body made people uneasy. "I am the Bread of Life," Jesus told a crowd. "My flesh is real food and my blood is true drink." People grew restless, disconcerted. "Does this shock you?" Jesus asked. It did.

In some ways, it would be more comforting to explain what goes on at Mass as mere symbolism. But the Catholic Church has always followed Jesus' lead, teaching that the consecrated bread and wine are transformed into Jesus' flesh and blood.

Exactly how the substance of bread and wine become the substance of Jesus' body is and always will be mystery. But then, so is the Incarnation. And isn't the mystery of the Eucharist in perfect continuity with the mystery of "God with us"? How consistent for a God who made a surprise appearance as a baby to continue his physical presence in an equally extraordinary way!

Something Greater Is Here
By Raniero Cantalamessa, OFMCap

One summer's day, I was celebrating Mass in a convent. The Gospel passage was Matthew 12; I shall never forget the impression these words of Jesus made on me: "Behold, something greater than Jonah is here.... Something greater than Solomon is here." Surely I was hearing them for the first time! I understood that the word "here" really meant here, in this precise place, at this precise moment, and not only when Jesus was on earth many centuries ago. A shudder ran through me and I was shaken out of my torpor: right there in front of me was something greater than Jonah, something greater than Solomon, than Abraham, than Moses: there was the Son of the living God! I understood the meaning of the words: "Lo I am with you always..." (Mt 28:20).

Ever since that summer's day, these words have become dear and familiar to me in a new way. Very often during Mass, when I genuflect after the Consecration I say to myself: "Behold, something greater than Jonah is here! Something greater than Solomon is here!"

———— —

Have Confidence: He Is Near
By Karl Rahner, SJ

He has come to us in our flesh and gives us this flesh because we do not know how to come to him. Because he is here, because he himself has come in the flesh of this earth, we want to receive the Bread of Life, his flesh which is our flesh, and we want to drink the cup of his Blood, in which our blood, the blood of our race, has been assumed and eternally redeemed. And because we feel so poor and empty, he gives us what is our own, where we are at home, what we understand, and calls it the pledge of his own divine life.

That is why we can always have confidence in him as our feelings tell us, and enter into this banquet of eternal life, because he is where we are and we have no cause to fear that he is far away; for he has given us his Body and Blood which are eternal life.

Kneeling Before Our God
Prayers of Adoration

꙰ꙮ꙰

May I never leave you there
alone but be wholly present,
my faith wholly vigilant,
wholly adoring,
and wholly surrendered to
your creative action.
    —*Blessed Elizabeth of the Trinity*

Prayer of Adoration
Adapted from Blessed James Alberione

Jesus, today's adoration is the meeting of my
   soul and all of my being with you.
I am the creature meeting the Creator;
the disciple before the Divine Master;
the patient with the Doctor of souls;
the poor one appealing to the Rich One;
the thirsty one drinking at the Font;
the weak before the Almighty;
the tempted seeking a sure Refuge;
the blind person searching for the Light;
the friend who goes to the True Friend;
the lost sheep sought by the Divine
   Shepherd;
the wayward heart who finds the Way;
the unenlightened one who finds Wisdom;
the bride who finds the Spouse of the soul;
the "nothing" who finds the All;
the afflicted who finds the Consoler;
the seeker who finds life's meaning.

Bone Pastor, Panis Vere
Traditional

Come then, good Shepherd, bread divine,
Still show to us thy mercy sign;
Oh, feed us, still keep us thine;
So we may see thy glories shine
In fields of immortality.
O thou, the wisest, mightiest, best,
Our present food, our future rest,
Come, make us each thy chosen guest,
Co-heirs of thine, and comrades blest
With saints whose dwelling is with thee.

We Remember
By Marty Haugen

We remember how you loved us to your death;
and still we celebrate, for you are with us
  here;
and we believe that we will see you
when you come in your glory, Lord.
We remember, we celebrate, we believe!

I Believe That You Accept Me
By Elizabeth Ruth Obbard, OCD

My God,
Jesus revealed you as a waiting Father
full of compassion and love
ever willing to welcome anyone who turns to
   you.
I believe that you accept me just as I am;
help me to accept myself.
I believe that your arms are open to receive
   me;
help me to cast myself into them.
I believe that you hear me even before I begin to pray
and that you know my heart's deepest
   desires.
You are with me here right now
loving me, forgiving me, finding joy in my
   being with you.
And so I can come to you with great confidence
knowing that all you want is my trust.

Bread of My Soul
By Venerable John Henry Newman

I place myself in the presence of him, in
   whose Incarnate Presence I am before I
   place myself there.
I adore you, my Savior, present here as God
   and man, in soul and body, in true flesh
   and blood.
I acknowledge and confess that I kneel before
   that sacred humanity, who was conceived
   in Mary's womb, and lay in Mary's bosom;
   who grew up to man's estate, and by the
   Sea of Galilee called the Twelve, wrought
   miracles, and spoke words of wisdom and
   peace; who in due season hung on the
   cross, lay in the tomb, rose from the dead,
   and now reigns in heaven.
I praise, and bless, and give myself wholly to
   him, who is the true Bread of my soul, and
   my everlasting joy.

O Sacred Banquet
By Saint Thomas Aquinas

O sacred banquet, in which we receive Christ;
we remember his passion;
we are filled with grace,
and we are given a pledge of future glory,
   alleluia!

———

I Keep the Lord Ever Before Me
Psalm 16:1–2, 3–8, 11

Protect me, O God, for in you I take refuge.
I say to the LORD, "You are my LORD;
   I have no good apart from you."

Those who choose another god multiply their
         sorrows;
      their drink offerings of blood I will not
         pour out
      or take their names upon my lips.

The LORD is my chosen portion and my cup;
   you hold my lot.
The boundary lines have fallen for me in
         pleasant places;
   I have a goodly heritage.

I bless the LORD who gives me counsel;
   in the night also my heart instructs me.
I keep the LORD always before me;
   because he is at my right hand,
     I shall not be moved.

You show me the path of life.
   In your presence there is fullness of joy;
   in your right hand are pleasures
     forevermore.

―――――

An Act of Love
By Saint John Vianney

I love you, O my God, and my only desire is to
love you until the last breath of my life. I love
you, O my infinitely lovable God, and I would
rather die loving you, than live without loving
you. I love you, Lord, and the only grace I ask
is to love you eternally.

   My God, if my tongue cannot say in every
moment that I love you, I want my heart to
repeat it to you as often as I draw breath.

―――――

Ave Verum

Traditional, adapted by Pope John Paul II

Ave verum corpus natum de Maria Virgine.
—Hail, true Body of Christ, born of the Virgin Mary!
The soul melts into wonder and adoration before so sublime a Mystery.

Vere passum, immolatum in cruce pro homine.
—Who truly suffered and was immolated on the cross for humanity.
From your death on the cross, O Lord, flows life for us which never dies.

Esto nobis praegustatum mortis in examine.
—May you be given as our food at the point of death.
O Lord, obtain that each one of us, nourished by you, may face all of life's trials with confident hope, until the day when you will be our viaticum for the last journey to the Father's house.

O Iesu dulcis! O Iesu pie! O Iesu, fili Mariae!
—O sweet Jesus, O merciful Jesus! O Jesus, Son of Mary! Amen!

Gloria Patri
Traditional

Glory to the Father, to the Son, and to the
  Holy Spirit,
as it was in the beginning, is now, and will
  be forever. Amen.

———— · ————

Immersed in Adoration
By Saint Faustina Kowalska

I adore you, Lord and Creator, hidden in the
Blessed Sacrament. I adore you for all the
works of your hands that reveal to me so
much wisdom, goodness, and mercy, O Lord.

You have spread so much beauty over the
earth, and it tells me about your beauty, even
though these beautiful things are but a faint
reflection of you, incomprehensible Beauty.

And although you have hidden yourself
and concealed your beauty, my eye, enlight-
ened by faith, reaches you and I recognize my
Creator, my highest Good, and my heart is
completely immersed in prayer of adoration.
(*Diary*, 1692)

———— · ————

Adore Te

By Saint Thomas Aquinas,
translated by Gerard Manley Hopkins

Godhead here in hiding, whom I do adore,
masked by these bare shadows, shape and
   nothing more;
see, Lord, at thy service low lies here a heart
lost, all lost in wonder at the God thou art.
Seeing, touching, tasting are in thee
   deceived;
how says trusty hearing? that shall be
   believed;
what God's Son has told me, take for truth I
   do;
Truth himself speaks truly or there's nothing
   true.
On the cross thy Godhead made no sign to
   men;
here thy very manhood steals from human
   ken:
both are my confession, both are my belief,
and I pray the prayer of the dying thief.
I am not like Thomas, wounds I cannot see,
but can plainly call thee Lord and God as he:
this faith each day deeper be my holding of,
daily make me harder hope and dearer love.

O thou our reminder of Christ crucified,
Living Bread the life of us for whom he died,
lend this life to me then: feed and feast my
 mind,
there be thou the sweetness man was meant
 to find.
Bring the tender tale true of the Pelican;
bathe me, Jesu Lord, in what thy bosom ran—
Blood that but one drop of has the world to
 win
all the world forgiveness of its world of sin.
Jesu whom I look at shrouded here below,
I beseech thee send me what I thirst for so,
some day to gaze on thee face to face in light
and be blest forever with thy glory's sight.

——— • ———

We Adore You
Attributed to Saint Francis of Assisi

We adore you, most holy Lord Jesus Christ,
here and in all your churches that are in the
whole world, and we bless you; because by
your holy cross you have redeemed the world.

——— • ———

Compassion
By Joan Metzner

Jesus, God, Spirit,
your compassionate love
fills my heart.
When other loves are tenuous,
your love remains changeless,
limitless,
beyond images.
Your compassion
has conquered suffering,
your love
is stronger than death.

———— ⋅ ————

Stay with Me, Lord
By Saint Pio of Pietrelcina

Stay with me, Lord, for it is necessary to have
you present so that I do not forget you.
Stay with me, Lord, because I am weak and I
need your strength, that I may not fall so
often.
Stay with me, Lord, for you are my life, and
without you, I am without fervor.
Stay with me, Lord, for you are my light, and
without you, I am in darkness.

Stay with me, Lord, to show me your will.

Stay with me, Lord, so that I hear your voice
and follow you.

Stay with me, Lord, for I desire to love you
very much, and always be in your company.

Stay with me, Lord, if you wish me to be
faithful to you.

Stay with me, Lord, for as poor as my soul is,
I wish it to be a place of consolation for
you, a nest of love....

Stay with me tonight, Jesus, in life with all its
dangers, I need you.

Let me recognize you as your disciples did at
the breaking of bread, so that Eucharistic
Communion may be the light which
disperses the darkness, the force which
sustains me, the unique joy of my heart....

Stay with me, Lord, for it is you alone I look
for. Your love, your grace, your will, your
heart, your Spirit, because I love you and
ask no other reward but to love you more
and more.

With a firm love, I will love you with all my
heart. Amen.

My Soul Is Thirsting for You
Psalm 63:1–8

O God, you are my God, I seek you,
  my soul thirsts for you;
my flesh faints for you,
  as in a dry and weary land
    where there is no water.
So I have looked upon you in the sanctuary,
  beholding your power and glory.
Because your steadfast love is better than life,
  my lips will praise you.
So I will bless you as long as I live;
  I will lift up my hands and call on
    your name.

My soul is satisfied as with a rich feast,
  and my mouth praises you with joyful lips
when I think of you on my bed,
  and meditate on you in the watches
    of the night;
for you have been my help,
  and in the shadow of your wings
    I sing for joy.
My soul clings to you;
  your right hand upholds me.

Prayer for Faith in the Real Presence
Traditional

We come to you, dear Lord, like the apostles, saying, "Increase our faith." Give us a strong and lively faith that you are really present in the Eucharist, a strong and active faith that we may live by.

Give us the splendid faith of the centurion, which drew such praise from you. Give us the faith of the beloved disciple to recognize you and say, "It is the Lord!" Give us the faith of Peter to confess, "You are Christ, the Son of the living God!" Give us the faith of Mary Magdalen to fall at your feet, crying, "Rabboni! Master!"

Give us the faith of all your saints to whom the Eucharist was heaven begun on earth. In every reception of the Eucharist and at every visit, increase our faith and love, our humility and reverence, and all good things will come to us.

Dearest Lord, increase our faith!

Companion of My Soul
By Henri J. M. Nouwen

Lord, I trust you; I entrust myself, with all my being, body, mind, and soul to you. I don't want to keep any secrets from you. You can see everything I do and hear everything I say. I don't want you to be a stranger any longer. I want you to become my most intimate friend.

I want you to know me, not only as I walk on the road and talk to my fellow travelers, but also as I find myself alone with my inner-most feelings and thoughts. And most of all, I want to come to know you, not just as my companion on the journey, but as the companion of my soul.

——— —

The Mirror
By Bernadette M. Reis, FSP

I am the soil, you are the seed;
I am the boat, you are the sea.
I am the branch, you are the vine;
I am the cup, you are the wine.
I am the clay, you the potter;
I am the dream, you the dreamer.
I am the earth, you are the rain;

I am the wood, you are the flame.
I am the bird, you are the wind;
I am the page, you are the print.
I am the pen, you are the hand;
I am the shore, you are the sand.
I am the dance, you are the song.
I am the image of you, my God.
So when I am weak, you make me strong.
For we are not two but one.

Beloved Jesus
By Patricia Shaules, FSP

Beloved Jesus, I believe that you are truly
present here in the Eucharist.
I adore you.
You look at me and listen to me as I look at
you and listen to you.
I love you.
You have given me everything that I am and
have. Thank you.
Please open my heart and mind so that our
visit together may be a time of union and
love and that I may be transformed into
you, my Teacher and Master. Amen.

Canticle from Saint Paul
Philippians 2:5–11

Let the same mind be in you that was in
   Christ Jesus,
who, though he was in the form of God,
   did not regard equality with God
   as something to be exploited,
but emptied himself,
   taking the form of a slave,
   being born in human likeness.
And being found in human form,
   he humbled himself
   and became obedient to the
      point of death—
   even death on a cross.

Therefore God also highly exalted him
   and gave him the name
   that is above every name,
so that at the name of Jesus
   every knee should bend,
   in heaven and on earth and under
      the earth,
and every tongue should confess
   that Jesus Christ is Lord,
   to the glory of God the Father.

Prayer of Surrender
By Venerable Charles de Foucauld

Father, I abandon myself into your hands;
do with me what you will.
Whatever you may do, I thank you;
I am ready for all, I accept all.
Let only your will be done in me,
and in all your creatures.
I wish no more than this, O Lord.
Into your hands I commend myself;
I offer myself to you with all the love
of my heart,
for I love you, Lord,
and so need to give myself,
to surrender myself into your hands
without reserve,
and with boundless confidence
for you are my Father.

You Have First Loved Me
Traditional, adapted

I adore you, Jesus, true God and true man, present here in the Holy Eucharist. United in spirit with all the faithful on earth and all the saints in heaven, I humbly kneel before you, in deepest gratitude for so great a blessing. I love you, my Jesus, with my whole heart, for you have first loved me.

May I never offend you by my lack of love. May your Eucharistic presence completely refresh me and lead me toward heaven. Mary, Mother of our Eucharistic Lord, pray for me and obtain for me a greater love for Jesus in the Eucharist. Amen.

Christ, Pouring Yourself Out
By Angela Ashwin

Christ, pouring yourself out,
love drained to the last drop,
I adore you.
Christ, kneeling as a servant, washing the
  disciples' feet,
shocking in your humility,

I adore you.
Christ, taking bread and wine,
crystal-clear in your awareness of the work
    you must complete,
I adore you.
Christ, entering Gethsemane, falling on your
    face to pray,
uncontainable in your broken heart,
I adore you.

A Spiritual Communion
By Saint Katharine Drexel

The Eucharist is a never-ending sacrifice. It is
the Sacrament of love, the act of love. Help
me each moment today and always to communicate myself to you by doing your will.
Let the doing of your will each moment be a
spiritual communion. In it you will give me
yourself; I will give you myself.

Behold the Beauty of the Lord
Psalm 27

The LORD is my light and my salvation;
   whom shall I fear?
The LORD is the stronghold of my life;
   of whom shall I be afraid?

When evildoers assail me
   to devour my flesh—
my adversaries and foes—
   they shall stumble and fall.

Though an army encamp against me,
   my heart shall not fear;
though war rise up against me,
   yet I will be confident.

One thing I asked of the LORD,
   that will I seek after:
to live in the house of the LORD
   all the days of my life,
to behold the beauty of the LORD,
   and to inquire in his temple.

For he will hide me in his shelter
   in the day of trouble;

he will conceal me under the cover
    of his tent;
  he will set me high on a rock.

Now my head is lifted up
  above my enemies all around me,
and I will offer in his tent
  sacrifices with shouts of joy;
I will sing and make melody to the LORD.

Hear, O LORD, when I cry aloud,
  be gracious to me and answer me!
"Come," my heart says, "seek his face!"
  Your face, LORD, do I seek.
  Do not hide your face from me.

Do not turn your servant away in anger,
  you who have been my help.
Do not cast me off, do not forsake me,
  O God of my salvation!
If my father and mother forsake me,
  the LORD will take me up.
Teach me your way, O LORD,
  and lead me on a level path
  because of my enemies.

Do not give me up to the will of
    my adversaries,
  for false witnesses have risen against me,
  and they are breathing out violence.

I believe that I shall see the goodness
    of the Lord
  in the land of the living.
Wait for the Lord;
  be strong, and let your heart take courage;
  wait for the Lord!

Delighting in His Presence

Prayers of Praise and Thanksgiving

ᖰᖰᖰ

**O memorial of the wonders
of God's love!**

—*Saint Katharine Drexel*

O Sacrament Most Holy
Traditional

O sacrament most holy, O sacrament divine!
All praise and all thanksgiving be every
   moment thine!

——— ———

Magnificat
Luke 1:46–55*

My soul gives praise to the Lord,
   and my spirit rejoices in God my Savior;
Because he had regard for the lowliness of
      his handmaid,
   behold, henceforth all generations shall
      call me blessed,
for the Mighty One has done great things
      for me,
   and holy is his name,
and his mercy is from generation to
      generation
   toward those who fear him.

He has shown might with his arm,
   scattered the arrogant in the conceit of
      their heart,
he has pulled down the mighty from
      their thrones,
   and exalted the lowly,
the hungry he has filled with good things,
   and the rich he has sent away empty.
He has come to the aid of his servant, Israel,
   mindful of his mercy,
just as he promised our fathers,
   Abraham and his descendants forever.

——— · ———

Act of Abandonment
By Venerable Thecla Merlo

You, O my God, always think of me.
You are within me, outside of me.
I am written on the palm of your hand.
O Lord, that I may always and in all things
do your will.
O Lord, I abandon myself in you.
No worries.
I abandon myself completely in you, always.

——— · ———

In Wonder
By Saint Teresa of Avila

O Wealth of the poor, how wonderfully can you sustain souls, revealing your great riches to them gradually and not permitting them to see them all at once! Since the time of that vision, I have never seen such great Majesty, hidden in a thing so small as the host, without marveling at your great wisdom.

O Immense Love!
By Saint Alphonsus de Liguori,
translated by Mary Emmanuel Alves, FSP

O my God, my true and only love, what more could you have done to win my love? It wasn't enough for you to die for me, you instituted the Blessed Sacrament to make yourself my food, that you might give yourself entirely to me, your creature.

O immense love! A God who gives himself totally to me! O my infinitely lovable God, I love you above all else, with all my heart.... In Communion you give yourself completely to me; now I give myself completely to you.

Thank You, Scandalous God
By Kate Compston

Thank you,
scandalous God,
for giving yourself to the world
not in the powerful and extraordinary
but in weakness and the familiar:
in a baby; in bread and wine.

Thank you
for offering, at journey's end,
    a new beginning;
for setting, in the poverty of a stable,
the richest jewel of your love;
for revealing, in a particular place,
your light for all nations....

Thank you
for bringing us to Bethlehem, House of Bread,
where the empty are filled,
where the filled are emptied;
where the poor find riches,
and the rich recognize their poverty;
where all who kneel and hold out
    their hands
are unstintingly fed.

Novena of Grace
Traditional Jesuit prayer

We give you thanks, O Lord, for all your
wondrous gifts.

We thank you for the gift of life: you called
us into being so that we might be your
children and live with you forever.

We thank you for our Baptism: you sealed us
with the Holy Spirit, gifted us with your
own life, grafted us into the mystical body
of your divine Son.

We thank you for our vocation to join with
the risen Christ in working to save and
sanctify the world in which we live.

We thank you for this Eucharist: you have fed
us on the Bread of Life, strengthened our
faith, renewed our hope, deepened our
love, made us one with one another in the
Body of Christ, our Lord.

We give you thanks, O Lord, for all your
wondrous gifts. Amen.

Praise of God's Love
By Alban Goodier, SJ

Lord, you loved me from all eternity, therefore you created me.

You loved me after you had made me, therefore you became man for me.

You loved me after you became man for me, therefore you lived and died for me.

You loved me after you had died for me, therefore you rose again for me.

You loved me after you had risen for me, therefore you went to prepare a place for me.

You loved me after you had gone to prepare a place for me, therefore you came back to me.

You loved me after you had come back to me, therefore you desire to enter into me and be united with me.

This is the meaning of the Eucharist, the mystery of love. Amen.

Happy Those Whose Strength Is You
Psalm 84:1–7, 10–12

How lovely is your dwelling place,
   O LORD of hosts!
My soul longs, indeed it faints
   for the courts of the LORD;
my heart and my flesh sing for joy
   to the living God.

Even the sparrow finds a home,
   and the swallow a nest for
         herself,
   where she may lay her young,
at your altars, O LORD of hosts,
   my King and my God.
Happy are those who live in your house,
   ever singing your praise.

Happy are those whose strength is in you,
   in whose heart are the highways to Zion.
As they go through the valley of Baca
   they make it a place of springs;
   the early rain also covers it with pools.
They go from strength to strength;
   the God of gods will be seen in Zion.

For a day in your courts is better
   than a thousand elsewhere.

I would rather be a doorkeeper in the
house of my God
than live in the tents of wickedness.

For the LORD God is a sun and shield;
he bestows favor and honor.
No good thing does the LORD withhold
from those who walk uprightly.
O LORD of hosts,
happy is everyone who trusts in you.

Bless God's Name!
Psalm 100:1–4

Make a joyful noise to the LORD, all the earth.
Worship the LORD with gladness;
come into his presence with singing.

Know that the LORD is God.
It is he that made us, and we are his;
we are his people, and the sheep
of his pasture.

Enter his gates with thanksgiving,
and his courts with praise.
Give thanks to him, bless his name.

Litany of the Eucharist

Lord, have mercy.
Lord, have mercy.

Christ, have mercy.
Christ, have mercy.

Lord, have mercy.
Lord, have mercy.

Jesus, the Most High,
R. Have mercy on us.

Jesus, the holy One, *R.*
Jesus, Word of God, *R.*
Jesus, only Son of the Father, *R.*
Jesus, Son of Mary, *R.*
Jesus, crucified for us, *R.*
Jesus, risen from the dead, *R.*
Jesus, our Lord, *R.*
Jesus, our hope, *R.*
Jesus, our peace, *R.*
Jesus, our Savior, *R.*
Jesus, our salvation, *R.*
Jesus, our resurrection, *R.*
Jesus, Lord of creation, *R.*
Jesus, lover of all, *R.*
Jesus, life of the world, *R.*

Jesus, freedom for the imprisoned, *R.*
Jesus, joy of the sorrowing, *R.*
Jesus, giver of the Spirit, *R.*
Jesus, giver of good gifts, *R.*
Jesus, source of new life, *R.*
Jesus, Lord of Life, *R.*
Jesus, true Shepherd, *R.*
Jesus, true Light, *R.*
Jesus, bread of heaven, *R.*
Jesus, Bread of Life, *R.*
Jesus, bread of thanksgiving, *R.*
Jesus, life-giving bread, *R.*
Jesus, holy manna, *R.*
Jesus, new covenant, *R.*
Jesus, food for everlasting life, *R.*
Jesus, food for our journey, *R.*
Jesus, holy banquet, *R.*
Jesus, true sacrifice, *R.*
Jesus, perfect sacrifice, *R.*
Jesus, eternal sacrifice, *R.*
Jesus, divine Victim, *R.*
Jesus, Mediator of the new Covenant, *R.*
Jesus, mystery of the altar, *R.*
Jesus, mystery of faith, *R.*
Jesus, medicine of immortality, *R.*
Jesus, pledge of eternal glory, *R.*

Jesus, Lamb of God,
you take away the sins of the world,
have mercy on us.

Jesus, bearer of our sins,
you take away the sins of the world,
have mercy on us.

Jesus, Redeemer of the world,
you take away the sins of the world:
have mercy on us.

Christ, hear us.
Christ, hear us.

Christ, graciously hear us.
Christ, graciously hear us.

Lord Jesus, hear our prayer.
Lord Jesus, hear our prayer.

Act of Faith, Hope, and Love in Jesus'
Eucharistic Presence
By Blessed James Alberione

Jesus, eternal Truth, we believe you are really
present in the Eucharist. You are here with
your Body, Blood, soul, and divinity. We hear

your invitation: "I am the living bread come down from heaven," "Take and eat; this is my body." We believe, O Lord and Master, but increase our faith.

Jesus, Way of salvation, you invite us: "Learn from me." But we resemble you so little! Lord, we are not worthy to receive you, but only say the word and we shall be healed. Jesus, you pleased the Father; you are our Way. Draw us to yourself, and give us the grace to love one another as you have loved us.

Jesus, our Life, our joy, and source of all good, we love you. We ask you that we may love you always more, and all those you have redeemed. You are the vine and we are the branches; we want to remain united to you always so as to bear much fruit. You are the source: pour out an ever-greater abundance of grace to sanctify us. You are the head and we are your members: communicate to us your Holy Spirit with all the Spirit's gifts. May your kingdom come through Mary. Amen.

Thanks Be to Thee
By Saint Richard of Chichester

Thanks be to thee, my Lord Jesus Christ,
for all the benefits
which thou hast given me,
O most merciful Friend,
Redeemer,
Brother.
May I see thee more clearly
love thee more dearly and
follow thee more nearly.

———

May We Live to Praise God's Glory
Ephesians 1:3–23

Blessed be the God and Father of our Lord Jesus Christ, who has blessed us in Christ with every spiritual blessing in the heavenly places, just as he chose us in Christ before the foundation of the world to be holy and blameless before him in love. He destined us for adoption as his children through Jesus Christ, according to the good pleasure of his will, to the praise of his glorious grace that he freely bestowed on us in the Beloved. In him we have redemption through his blood, the forgiveness of our trespasses, according to the riches of his grace that he lavished on us.

With all wisdom and insight he has made known to us the mystery of his will, according to his good pleasure that he set forth in Christ, as a plan for the fullness of time, to gather up all things in him, things in heaven and things on earth. In Christ we have also obtained an inheritance, having been destined according to the purpose of him who accomplishes all things according to his counsel and will, so that we, who were the first to set our hope on Christ, might live for the praise of his glory.

Fed by Your Bounty
By Jarena Lee

Lord, I have been fed with your bounty,
clothed with your mercy.
comforted by your love,
healed by your grace,
and upheld by your hand.

Believe in Him and Rejoice with Joy
1 Peter 1:3–9

Blessed be the God and Father of our Lord Jesus Christ! By his great mercy he has given us
a new birth into a living hope through the
resurrection of Jesus Christ from the dead,
and into an inheritance that is imperishable,
undefiled, and unfading, kept in heaven for
you, who are being protected by the power of
God through faith for a salvation ready to be
revealed in the last time. In this you rejoice,
even if now for a little while you have had to
suffer various trials, so that the genuineness
of your faith—being more precious than gold
that, though perishable, is tested by fire—
may be found to result in praise and glory
and honor when Jesus Christ is revealed. Although you have not seen him, you love him;
and even though you do not see him now, you
believe in him and rejoice with an indescrib-
able and glorious joy, for you are receiving
the outcome of your faith, the salvation of
your souls.

I Fear Nothing, For You Are Here
Psalm 23

The LORD is my shepherd, I shall not want.
  He makes me lie down in green pastures;
he leads me beside still waters;
  he restores my soul.
He leads me in right paths
  for his name's sake.

Even though I walk through the darkest
      valley,
  I fear no evil;
for you are with me;
  your rod and your staff—
  they comfort me.

You prepare a table before me
  in the presence of my enemies;
you anoint my head with oil;
  my cup overflows.
Surely goodness and mercy shall follow me
  all the days of my life
and I shall dwell in the house of the LORD
  my whole life long.

Hymn of Thanksgiving
By Saint Faustina Kowalska

O Jesus, eternal God, thank you for your countless graces and blessings. Let every beat of my heart be a new hymn of thanksgiving to you, O God. Let every drop of my blood circulate for you, Lord. My soul is one hymn in adoration of your mercy. I love you, God, for yourself alone (*Diary*, 1794).

———————

Who Will Separate Us from Christ?
Romans 8:31–39

If God is for us, who is against us? He who did not withhold his own Son, but gave him up for all of us, will he not with him also give us everything else? Who will bring any charge against God's elect? It is God who justifies. Who is to condemn? It is Christ Jesus, who died, yes, who was raised, who is at the right hand of God, who indeed intercedes for us. Who will separate us from the love of Christ? Will hardship, or distress, or persecution, or famine, or nakedness, or peril, or sword? As it is written,

"For your sake we are being killed all day long; we are accounted as sheep to be slaughtered."

No, in all these things we are more than conquerors through him who loved us. For I am convinced that neither death, nor life, nor angels, nor rulers, nor things present, nor things to come, nor powers, nor height, nor depth, nor anything else in all creation, will be able to separate us from the love of God in Christ Jesus our Lord.

Encountering Merciful Love
Prayers for Conversion and Healing

࿔

'God conquers evil with infinite
mercy. It is in the face of this
merciful love that a desire
for conversion and a yearning
for new life must be
reawakened in us.

—*Pope John Paul II*

The Lord Has Compassion on Us
Psalm 103:1–5, 13–18

Bless the LORD, O my soul,
    and all that is within me,
    bless his holy name.
Bless the LORD, O my soul,
    and do not forget all his benefits—
who forgives all your iniquity,
    who heals all your diseases,
who redeems your life from the Pit,
    who crowns you with steadfast
        love and mercy,
who satisfies you with good as
        long as you live
    so that your youth is renewed
        like the eagle's.

As a father has compassion for his children,
    so the LORD has compassion
        for those who fear him.
For he knows how we were made;
    he remembers that we are dust.

As for mortals, their days are like grass;
  they flourish like a flower of the field;
for the wind passes over it, and it is gone,
  and its place knows it no more.
But the steadfast love of the LORD is from
      everlasting to everlasting
  on those who fear him,
  and his righteousness to children's children,
to those who keep his covenant
  and remember to do his commandments.

——— · ———

Be Merciful
Traditional

Be merciful,
O Lord,
for we have sinned.

——— · ———

To Jesus, Good Shepherd
Adapted from Blessed James Alberione

Jesus, you are the Good Shepherd
who gathers and cares
for the scattered sheep.
The shepherd leads
and the sheep follow
because they recognize the shepherd's voice.
You have given your commandments,
your counsels, your examples.
Whoever heeds them is nourished
with bread that does not perish:
"My food is to do the will of the
   heavenly Father."
Have mercy on us when we try to
   nourish ourselves
on falsehood or empty pleasures.
Recall us to your way.
Sustain us when we waver, strengthen us
   when we are weak.
May everyone follow you,
Shepherd and Guardian of our souls.
You alone are the Way,
you alone have words of eternal life.
We will follow you wherever you go. Amen.

Lord, You Placed Me Here

By Peggy M. de Cuehlo

Lord, you placed me in the world to be
    its salt.
I was afraid of committing myself, afraid of
    being stained by the world.
I did not want to hear what "they" might say.
And my salt dissolved as if in water.
Forgive me, Jesus.
Lord, you placed me in the world to be
    its light.
I was afraid of the shadows, afraid of
    the poverty.
I did not want to know other people.
And my light slowly faded away.
Forgive me, Jesus.
Lord, you placed me in the world to live
    in community.
Thus you taught me to love,
to share in life,
to struggle for bread and for justice,
your truth incarnate in my life.
So be it, Jesus.

Grant Me Your Steadfast Love
Psalm 51:1–17

Have mercy on me, O God,
   according to your steadfast love;
according to your abundant mercy
   blot out my transgressions.
Wash me thoroughly from my iniquity,
   and cleanse me from my sin.

For I know my transgressions,
   and my sin is ever before me.
Against you, you alone, have I sinned,
   and done what is evil in your sight,
so that you are justified in your sentence
   and blameless when you pass judgment.
Indeed, I was born guilty,
   a sinner when my mother conceived me.
You desire truth in the inward being;
      therefore teach me wisdom in my secret
         heart.
Purge me with hyssop, and I shall be clean;
   wash me, and I shall be whiter than snow.
Let me hear joy and gladness;
   let the bones you have crushed rejoice.
Hide your face from my sins,
   and blot out all my iniquities.

Create in me a clean heart, O God,
   and put a new and right spirit within me.
Do not cast me away from your presence,
   and do not take your holy spirit from me.
Restore to me the joy of your salvation,
   and sustain in me a willing spirit.
Then I will teach transgressors your ways,
   and sinners will return to you.
Deliver me from bloodshed, O God,
   O God of my salvation,
   and my tongue will sing aloud of your
      deliverance.

O Lord, open my lips,
   and my mouth will declare your praise.
For you have no delight in sacrifice;
   if I were to give a burnt offering,
      you would not be pleased.
The sacrifice acceptable to God is
      a broken spirit;
   a broken and contrite heart,
      O God, you will not despise.

Drawing Near to You
By Saint Thomas Aquinas

Almighty and eternal God, I approach the sacrament of your only-begotten Son, our Lord Jesus Christ. I am sick and draw near to the Physician of life; unclean to the Fountain of mercy; blind to the Light of eternal brightness; poor and needy to the Lord of heaven and earth.

I ask you, in your abundant goodness, to heal my sickness, cleanse my sinfulness, enlighten my blindness, enrich my poverty, and clothe my nakedness.

Make me ready to receive the Bread of angels, the King of kings, and Lord of Lords, with reverence and humility, contrition and love, purity and faith, with the purpose and intention necessary for the good of my soul.... Grant that I may be worthy to be incorporated into his Mystical Body and counted among his members.

Good Friday
By Bernadette M. Reis, FSP

I so want to belong to you totally, Jesus,
in my thoughts and words and deeds.
But I see my frailty and weakness
   and sinfulness.
Let me allow you, Jesus,
to love me because I am weak and sinful
   and poor,
not because I am perfect.
Help me to embrace my pain, humanity,
   and sorrow
so that in your love, Jesus,
they may become my joy and hope
   and wealth.
Let me appear as a child before you, Jesus,
helpless—yet knowing that you would never
   refuse me your love.
Let me be yours forever, Jesus,
and you will always be mine. Amen.

To Return to You
By Francis Xavier Nguyen Van Thuan

Lord, grant me the strength to return to you,
like the prodigal son.
You are the principle of my life
and no one knows as well as you
what is most useful to me.
You have traced a path for each of us
in the plan of your love.
At each instant, we want to offer you
   our will.
In spite of ourselves,
we will not merely be resigned,
but as your children we will be always
   available to your plan for us.
May your will be ours!

The Jesus Prayer
Traditional

Lord Jesus Christ,
Son of David,
have mercy on me
a sinner.

Repentance and Reunion
By Saint Hildegard of Bingen

Father, I have sinned against heaven
  and myself,
though you created me as your divine work.
Formed and touched by you,
my actions should have been divine.
Because I violated my own human nature,
I have also sinned before you.
Self-inflicted misery is my downfall.
I am no longer worthy of being called
  your child,
because I have alienated myself
of my own free will
from your creation within me—
the way you have prepared.
Now treat me as your servant,
whose freedom you paid at a high price
in the blood of your Son.
Through Adam the inheritance of your
  children was lost to me.
But now repentance shall repay the debt of
  my sins
with the blood of your Son.

———

Hope In the Lord!
Psalm 130:1–7a

Out of the depths I cry to you, O LORD.
 LORD, hear my voice!
Let your ears be attentive
 to the voice of my supplications!

If you, O LORD, should mark iniquities,
 Lord, who could stand?
But there is forgiveness with you,
 so that you may be revered.

I wait for the LORD, my soul waits,
 and in his word I hope;
my soul waits for the LORD
 more than those who watch for
  the morning,
 more than those who watch for
  the morning.

 O Israel, hope in the LORD!

Love (III)
By George Herbert

Love bade me welcome: yet my soul drew
    back,
  Guilty of dust and sin.
But quick-ey'd Love, observing me
    grow slack
  From my first entrance in,
Drew nearer to me, sweetly questioning,
  If I lack'd anything.

A guest, I answer'd, worthy to be here:
  Love said, You shall be he.
I, the unkind, ungrateful? Ah, my dear,
  I cannot look on thee.
Love took my hand, and smiling did reply,
  Who made the eyes but I?

Truth, Lord, but I have marr'd them:
    let my shame
  Go where it doth deserve.
And know you not, says Love, who bore
    the blame?
  My dear, then I will serve.
You must sit down, says Love, and taste
    my meat:
  So I did sit and eat.

You Deliver Me, O Lord
Psalm 32:1–7, 11

Happy are those whose transgression
     is forgiven,
  whose sin is covered.
Happy are those to whom the LORD imputes
     no iniquity,
  and in whose spirit there is no deceit.

While I kept silence, my body wasted away
  through my groaning all day long.
For day and night your hand was heavy
     upon me;
  my strength was dried up as by the heat
    of summer.

Then I acknowledged my sin to you,
  and I did not hide my iniquity;
I said, "I will confess my transgressions to
    the LORD,"
  and you forgave the guilt of my sin.

Therefore let all who are faithful offer prayer
     to you;
  at a time of distress, the rush of
     mighty waters
  shall not reach them.

You are a hiding place for me;
  you preserve me from trouble;
  you surround me with glad cries
      of deliverance.
Be glad in the LORD and rejoice, O righteous,
  and shout for joy, all you upright in heart.

Beyond Ourselves
By Kate McIlhagga

Lord of the unexpected moment,
Christ the surprising,
why do we always
try to own you,
mistake reality for dream,
shut the door on the impossible?

Calm our fears,
shatter the walls we build
to keep you out.
Confront our hypocrisy.
Catch us when we fail.
Son of God,
save us from ourselves.

To Jesus Crucified
Traditional

Behold, my beloved and good Jesus,
I kneel before you,
asking you most earnestly
to engrave upon my heart
a deep and lively faith, hope, and charity,
with true repentance for my sins,
and a firm resolve to make amends.
As I reflect upon your five wounds,
and dwell upon them with deep compassion
    and grief,
I recall, good Jesus, the words the prophet
    David spoke long ago:
They have pierced my hands and my feet,
they have counted all my bones!

Possess Our Hearts
By Saint Augustine of Hippo

Lord Jesus, our Savior,
let us now come to you.
Our hearts are cold; Lord, warm them with
   your selfless love.
Our hearts are sinful; Lord, cleanse them
   with your precious blood.
Our hearts are weak; Lord, strengthen them
   with your joyous spirit.
Our hearts are empty; Lord, fill them with
   your divine presence.
Lord Jesus, our hearts are yours; possess
   them always and only for yourself.
Amen.

——— ———

Litany of the Sacred Heart of Jesus
Traditional

Lord, have mercy on us.
Christ, have mercy on us.

Lord, have mercy on us. Christ, hear us.
Christ, graciously hear us.

God the Father of heaven,
R. Have mercy on us.

God the Son, Redeemer of the world, *R.*
God the Holy Spirit, *R.*
Holy Trinity, one God, *R.*

Heart of Jesus, formed by the Holy Spirit in
the womb of the Virgin Mother, *R.*
Heart of Jesus, substantially united to the
Word of God, *R.*
Heart of Jesus, of infinite majesty, *R.*
Heart of Jesus, sacred temple of God, *R.*
Heart of Jesus, tabernacle of the
Most High, *R.*
Heart of Jesus, burning furnace of charity, *R.*
Heart of Jesus, abode of justice and love, *R.*
Heart of Jesus, full of goodness and love, *R.*
Heart of Jesus, abyss of all virtues, *R.*
Heart of Jesus, most worthy of all praises, *R.*

Heart of Jesus, King and center of
all hearts, *R.*

Heart of Jesus, in whom are all the treasures
of wisdom and knowledge, *R.*

Heart of Jesus, in whom dwells the fullness
of divinity, *R.*

Heart of Jesus, in whom the Father was well
pleased, *R.*

Heart of Jesus, of whose fullness we have all
received, *R.*

Heart of Jesus, desire of the everlasting
hills, *R.*

Heart of Jesus, patient and most merciful, *R.*

Heart of Jesus, enriching all who invoke
you, *R.*

Heart of Jesus, fountain of life and
holiness, *R.*

Heart of Jesus, wounded for our sins, *R.*

Heart of Jesus, laden with insults, *R.*

Heart of Jesus, bruised for our offenses, *R.*

Heart of Jesus, obedient unto death, *R.*

Heart of Jesus, pierced with a lance, *R.*

Heart of Jesus, source of all consolation, *R.*

Heart of Jesus, our life and resurrection, *R.*

Heart of Jesus, our peace and
reconciliation, *R.*

Heart of Jesus, salvation of those who trust in
 you, *R.*
Heart of Jesus, hope of those who die
 in you, *R.*
Heart of Jesus, delight of all the saints, *R.*

Lamb of God, you take away the sins of the
 world, *spare us, O Lord.*
Lamb of God, you take away the sins of the
 world, *graciously hear us, O Lord.*

Lamb of God, you take away the sins of the
 world,
have mercy on us.

Jesus, meek and humble of heart,
make our hearts like yours.

Let us pray. Father, we rejoice in the gifts of
love we have received from the heart of Jesus
your Son. Open our hearts to share his life
and continue to bless us with his love. We ask
this in the name of Jesus the Lord. Amen.

Act of Contrition
Traditional

My God,
I am sorry for my sins with all my heart.
In choosing to do wrong
and failing to do good,
I have sinned against you
whom I should love above all things.
I firmly intend, with your help,
to do penance,
to sin no more,
and to avoid whatever leads me to sin.
Our Savior Jesus Christ
suffered and died for us.
In his name, my God, have mercy.

Guidelines for Celebrating the Sacrament of Reconciliation

The two sacraments of the Eucharist and Penance are very closely connected. Because the Eucharist makes present the redeeming sacrifice of the cross, perpetuating it sacramentally, it naturally gives rise to a continuous need for conversion, for a personal response to the appeal made by Saint Paul to the Christians of Corinth: "We beseech you on behalf of Christ, be reconciled to God" (2 Cor 5:20).

—Pope John Paul II

To receive this sacrament and spiritually benefit from it, a person needs:

1. To examine his or her conscience;

2. To be sincerely sorry for sin;

3. To resolve to avoid sin in the future;

4. To confess the sins committed;

5. To accept the penance assigned.

Counsels for Living a Christian Life
The Ten Commandments (cf. Exodus 20:1–17)

I am the Lord your God:

1. You shall not have other gods besides me.

2. You shall not take the name of the Lord your God in vain.

3. Remember to keep holy the Lord's day.

4. Honor your father and your mother.

5. You shall not kill.

6. You shall not commit adultery.

7. You shall not steal.

8. You shall not bear false witness against your neighbor.

9. You shall not covet your neighbor's wife.

10. You shall not covet your neighbor's goods.

The Beatitudes
Matthew 5:3–12

"Blessed are the poor in spirit, for theirs is the kingdom of heaven.

"Blessed are those who mourn, for they will be comforted.

"Blessed are the meek, for they will inherit the earth.

"Blessed are those who hunger and thirst for righteousness, for they will be filled.

"Blessed are the merciful, for they will receive mercy.

Blessed are the pure in heart, for they will see God.

"Blessed are the peacemakers, for they will be called children of God.

"Blessed are those who are persecuted for righteousness' sake, for theirs is the kingdom of heaven.

"Blessed are you when people revile you and persecute you and utter all kinds of evil against you falsely on my account. Rejoice and be glad, for your reward is great in heaven, for in the same way they persecuted the prophets who were before you."

Drawing Near in Confidence

Petitions and Prayers
for Personal Transformation

❧❧❧

I do not pray for success.
I pray for faithfulness.

—Blessed Teresa of Calcutta

You Know My Heart, O God
Psalm 139

O LORD, you have searched me and known
      me.
You know when I sit down and when
       I rise up;
  you discern my thoughts from far away.
You search out my path and my lying down,
   and are acquainted with all my ways.
Even before a word is on my tongue,
   O LORD, you know it completely.
You hem me in, behind and before,
   and lay your hand upon me.
Such knowledge is too wonderful for me;
   it is so high that I cannot attain it.

Where can I go from your spirit?
   Or where can I flee from your presence?
If I ascend to heaven, you are there;
   if I make my bed in Sheol, you are there.
If I take the wings of the morning
   and settle at the farthest limits of the sea,

even there your hand shall lead me,
and your right hand shall hold me fast.
If I say, "Surely the darkness shall cover me,
and the light around me become night,"
even the darkness is not dark to you;
the night is as bright as the day,
for darkness is as light to you.

For it was you who formed my inward parts;
you knit me together in my mother's womb.
I praise you, for I am fearfully and
wonderfully made.
Wonderful are your works;
that I know very well.
My frame was not hidden from you,
when I was being made in secret,
intricately woven in the depths of
the earth.
Your eyes beheld my unformed substance.
In your book were written
all the days that were formed for me,
when none of them as yet existed.
How weighty to me are your thoughts,
O God!
How vast is the sum of them!

I try to count them—they are more than
    the sand;
  I come to the end—I am still with you.

O that you would kill the wicked, O God,
    and that the bloodthirsty would depart
        from me—
those who speak of you maliciously,
    and lift themselves up against you for evil!
Do I not hate those who hate you, O LORD?
    And do I not loathe those who rise up
        against you?
I hate them with perfect hatred;
    I count them my enemies.
Search me, O God, and know my heart;
    test me and know my thoughts.
See if there is any wicked way in me,
    and lead me in the way everlasting.

Deepen My Faith
By Henri J. M. Nouwen

Dear Lord, on this day dedicated to the Eu-
    charist,
  I think of the thousands of people suffering
    from lack of food and of the millions suf-
    fering from lack of love.

While I am well fed and well cared for,
while I am enjoying the fruits of the earth
   and the love of the brothers,
I am aware of the physical and emotional
   destitution
of so many of my fellow human beings.
Isn't my faith in your presence in the breaking of the bread
meant to reach out beyond the small circle of
   my brothers
to the larger circle of humanity
and to alleviate suffering as much as
   possible?
If I can recognize you in the Sacrament of
   the Eucharist
I must also be able to recognize you in the
   many hungry men, women, and children.
If I cannot translate my faith in your
   presence under the appearance of bread
   and wine
into action for the world
I am still an unbeliever.
I pray, therefore, Lord,
deepen my faith in your Eucharistic presence
and help me find ways to let this faith bear
   fruit in the lives of many. Amen.

Satisfy Our Hunger, Lord
By David M. Turoldo

We implore the Father,
who in his Son Jesus Christ gave us the food
  of immortality,
and we say: *Satisfy our hunger, Lord.*

Merciful Father, you have never abandoned
  your people in times of anguish and
  distress.
—As in the desert you sent manna to satisfy
  the hunger of the dying, so always help
  your Church with the food of eternal life.

Merciful Father, you did not forget Elijah in
  his desperation, but sent him an angel with
  the food that would sustain him to the
  mountain of your presence.
—Give also to us the bread that strengthens,
  so we may continue to journey toward the
  Day of meeting you.

Merciful Father, you rewarded the faith of
  the widow of Zarephath with bread and oil
  until the end of the great famine.
—Strengthen our weak faith, so we will not
  despair in time of trial.

Merciful Father, your Son Jesus multiplied bread for the hungry crowds, but in the desert he resisted the temptation to transform stones into bread.

—Free us from the danger of making material interests a priority; help us to live only by your Word.

Merciful Father, when the hour came for Jesus to die for us, he left his disciples a sign as a perpetual remembrance of him: the broken bread and the wine of the new covenant.

—Grant that we who eat his Body and drink his Blood may also be for our brothers and sisters a bread that gives life and a chalice that radiates glory.

——— —

Gift of Contemplation
By William Blake

To see a world in a grain of sand
and a heaven in a wildflower,
hold Infinity in the palm of your hand
and Eternity in an hour.

——— —

Let My Work Be Gift
By Francis Xavier Nguyen Van Thuan

Lord, teach me the virtues of work:
the patience of a sculptor modeling a statue,
of a weaver making a blanket,
or of a seamstress bent over fabric.
Teach me the vivacity of a young person at a
    computer,
the perseverance of a farmer in a field,
the tenacity of a mechanic repairing a car,
the dignity of a mother cooking for her family,
the tenderness of a nurse.
If I cherish my occupation
and respect those I serve and yet do not
    know,
smiling and showing my satisfaction
and joy from the depths of my heart,
offering the fruit of my labor for others' use,
then all I do becomes my work,
and my life will be a gift
offered to the Lord through those I
    encounter.

Shine Through Me
By Venerable John Henry Newman

Dear Jesus, help me to spread your fragrance everywhere I go. Flood my soul with your Spirit and life. Penetrate and possess my whole being so utterly that my life may only be a radiance of yours.

Shine through me and be so in me that every person I come in contact with may feel your presence in my soul. Let them look up, and see no longer me, but only Jesus! Stay with me and then I shall begin to shine as you shine, so to shine as to be a light to others. The light, Jesus, will be all from you; none of it will be mine. It will be you shining on others through me. Let me thus praise you in the way which you love best, by shining on those around me.

Let me preach you without preaching, not by my words but by my example, by the catching force, the sympathetic influence of what I do, the evident fullness of the love my heart bears for you. Amen.

———

Forever Yours
By Bernadette M. Reis, FSP

Father,
You have given us infinity
and all things flow from your hands—
from the vast reaches of the galaxies
to the smallest grains of sand.
All creation chants your praise
in silence, sight and sound adore!
Cradled in the arms of your embrace:
We are forever yours.

Jesus,
When our sins shrouded us in shadows
our eyes beheld despair.
We spurned all signs of your love below—
you, the fullness of God's care.
Yet you drew us to your embrace—
upon the cross our hope restored.
Lifted in the light of your loving gaze:
We are forever yours.

Holy Spirit,
Hidden guide dwelling deep within the soul.
Wordlessly you awaken the thirst
for that home where the broken are made
   whole.

As calm covers the crashing surf
we yield to your embrace;
as you beacon us to safe harbor
in the intimacy of your grace:
We are forever yours.

Body of Christ,
We hold this awesome, boundless treasure
to be poured out on the world.
Behold these gifts of splendor—
his precious, priceless pearls!
And with our lives we trace
the pattern of God's love so all will know
the infinite riches of his grace:
We are forever yours.

Prayer of Judith
Judith 9:11–12

You are the God of the lowly, helper of the
oppressed, upholder of the weak, protector
of the forsaken, savior of those without hope.
Please, please, God of my father, God of the
heritage of Israel, Lord of heaven and earth,
Creator of the waters, King of all your creation, hear my prayer!

O Living Bread!
By Blessed Pope John XXIII

O living Bread,
who came down from heaven to give life to
    the world!
O loving Shepherd of souls, a hidden God,
who pours out your grace
on families and peoples,
we commend to you
particularly those who are sick, unhappy,
    poor,
and all who beg for food and employment,
imploring for all and everyone the assistance
    of your providence;
we commend to you the families
so that they may be fruitful centers of
    Christian life.
May the abundance of your grace be poured
    over all.

Anima Christi
Traditional

Soul of Christ, sanctify me.
Body of Christ, save me.

Blood of Christ, inebriate me.
Water flowing from the side of Christ,
  wash me.
Passion of Christ, strengthen me.
Good Jesus, hear me.
Within your wounds, hide me
and keep me close to thee.
From the evil enemy defend me.
In the hour of my death, call me
and bid me come to thee,
that with thy saints I may praise thee
through all eternity.

——— ———

Purge Our Eyes
By Christina Rossetti

Lord, purge our eyes to see
within the seed a tree,
within the glowing egg a bird,
within the shroud a butterfly.
Till, taught by such we see
beyond all creatures, thee
and hearken to thy tender word
and hear its "Fear not, it is I."

——— ———

Love of Jesus
By Angela Ashwin

Love of Jesus, fill me.
Joy of Jesus, surprise me.
Peace of Jesus, flood me.
Light of Jesus, transform me.
Touch of Jesus, warm me.
Strength of Jesus, encourage me.

O Savior, in your agony, forgive me,
in your wounds, hide me,
and in your risen life take me with you,
to share in your life everlasting. Amen.

Morning Offering
By Saint Thérèse of Lisieux

My God, I offer you all that I do today for the intentions and the glory of the Sacred Heart of Jesus. I want to sanctify every beat of my heart, my thoughts, and my simplest works by uniting them to his infinite merits. I want to repair for my faults by casting them into the furnace of his merciful love.

O my God! I ask you for myself and those dear to me the grace to fulfill perfectly your holy will and to accept for love of you the joys and sorrows of this passing life so that one day we may be reunited in heaven for all eternity. Amen.

———

A Family Prayer
By Robert Louis Stevenson

Lord, behold our family.
We thank you for this place in which we
    dwell,
for the love that unites us,
for the peace accorded us this day,
for the hope with which we expect the mor-
    row;
for the health, the work, the food, and the
    bright skies
that make our lives delightful;
for our friends in all parts of the earth.
    Amen.

———

Litany of Service
Based on Isaiah 42, 49, 50, and 52

Lord, I believe that I am your chosen servant
whom you uphold.
Send your spirit upon me.
Lord, I believe that you have taken me by the
hand and formed me.
Make me a light for those in darkness.
Lord, I believe you called me before I was
born and named me.
*Make me your faithful servant through whom
you will be glorified.*
Lord, sometimes I think I have worked in
vain and that I have spent my strength for
nothing.
*Help me remember that you are my strength
and my reward is in you.*
Lord, each morning you open my ears that I
may hear and speak your words: comfort to
the weary, encouragement to those who are
oppressed.
The Lord God helps me.
Lord, I offer whatever I suffer as a way to
share in the hardships suffered by your
people.

*Give me the peace of surrender to your will
and the courage to oppose oppression.*

———————

Is My Life Too "Safe," O Lord?
By Francis Xavier Nguyen Van Thuan

Grant, Lord, that we may offer
the Eucharistic sacrifice with great love.

If we do not offer ourselves with Jesus in
   some way,
if our lives are safe from hunger, thirst, cold,
   and humiliation;
if our faces are not struck by slaps and spittle;
if a crown of thorns is not inflicted upon us;
if we do not carry the cross, are not nailed to
   it,
do not die on it;
and if we are not buried in another's tomb,
then we must be transformed.
If because of fear I try to escape Jesus' destiny,
then despite all the rites I follow and their
   solemnity,
I am not offering the Eucharistic sacrifice
with Jesus' sentiments.

———————

Live in Me, Jesus Master
Adapted from Blessed James Alberione

Master, your life traces out the path for me; your teachings confirm and light up my steps; your grace strengthens and sustains me along the journey to heaven. You are the perfect Master. You teach and give example and encouragement to us, the disciples who follow you.

Master, you have the words of eternal life. Transform my mind and my thoughts with yours. You enlighten every person, and you are Truth itself; I want to reason things out only as you taught, to think as you think. Live in my mind, O Jesus Truth.

Your life is way, the only secure and true way. In the stable, at Nazareth, on Calvary, you traced out for us the divine path of love for the Father, of love for humanity to the point of total sacrifice. Make me know your way, and in every moment may I be able to place my feet in your footsteps. Any other way is wide and is not your way. I want what you want; transform my will into yours.

Transform my heart with your heart. Transform my love of God, of self, and of neighbor, with your love. Transform my sinful human life with your divine life. May this life manifest itself in all I do. "May the life of Christ be manifest in my body," as it was in Saint Paul, who said: "Christ lives in me." Live in me, O Jesus, eternal and substantial Life.

As I Walk in Your Light
By Venerable John Henry Newman

Jesus in the Eucharist,
give me the grace of a cheerful heart,
an even temper, sweetness,
gentleness, and brightness of mind
as I walk in your light and by your grace.
I pray you to give me the spirit
of over-abundant, ever-springing love,
which overpowers the vexations of life
by its own riches and strength
and which, above all things, unites me to you
who are the fountain and the center of all
   mercy, loving kindness, and joy. Amen.

Suscipe
By Saint Ignatius of Loyola

Take, Lord, and receive all my liberty,
my memory, my understanding,
and my entire will,
all I have and call my own.

You have given all to me.
To you, Lord, I return it.

Everything is yours; do with it what you will.
Give me only your love and your grace,
that is enough for me.

Blessing Prayer for Healing
By Joyce Rupp

If praying for another, insert "you" in place of "I."

May I desire to be healed.
May what is wounded in my life be restored
   to good health.
May I be receptive to the ways in which heal~
   ing needs to happen.
May I take good care of myself.
May I extend compassion to all that hurts
   within my body, mind, spirit.

May I be patient with the time it takes to
  heal.

May I be aware of the wonders of my body,
  mind, and spirit, and their amazing capacity to heal.

May the skills of all those who care for me be
  used to the best of their ability in return-
  ing me to good health.

May I be open to receive from those who extend kindness, care, and compassion.

May I rest peacefully under the sheltering
  wings of divine love, trusting in this gracious presence.

May I find little moments of beauty and joy
  to sustain me.

May I keep hope in my heart.

*Hold your hands over your own heart, and accept the
power of love within you.*

Creed of Those Who Are Called
From the Pauline Letters

We believe that God chose us in him before
  the world began, to be holy and blameless
  in his sight.

We believe that those whom he foreknew he
  predestined to share the image of his Son.

We believe that God who had set us apart
  before we were born and called us by his
  favor chose to reveal his Son to us, that we
  might spread among all people the good
  tidings concerning him.

We believe that God has saved us and has
  called us to a holy life, not because of any
  merit of ours, but according to his own
  design—the grace held out to us in Christ
  Jesus before the world began.

We believe that Christ Jesus has judged us
  faithful and worthy by calling us to his
  service.

We believe that we are apostles by vocation,
  servants of Christ Jesus, set apart to
  announce the Gospel of God.

Considering our vocation, we believe that
  God chose the weak of this world to shame
  the strong, so that our faith would not rest
  on the wisdom of men but on the power of
  God.

We believe that to each one God has given
  the manifestation of the Spirit for the common good.

We believe that we must live a life worthy of
the calling which we have received, with
perfect humility, meekness, and patience,
seeking to grow in all things toward him.

We believe that all things work together for
the good of those who love God, who have
been called according to his decree.

We believe in him whose power now at work
in us can do immeasurably more than we
ask or imagine.

We believe that he who has begun the good
work in us will carry it through to comple-
tion, right up to the day of Christ Jesus,
because he who calls us is faithful.

Invocations to Jesus Master
By Blessed James Alberione

Jesus Master, sanctify my mind and increase
my faith.

Jesus, teaching in the Church, draw everyone
to yourself.

Jesus Master, deliver me from error, empty
thoughts, and eternal blindness.

Jesus, Way between the Father and us, I offer
you everything and await all from you.

Jesus, Way of sanctity, help me imitate you
  faithfully.

Jesus Way, may I respond wholeheartedly to
  the Father's call to holiness.

Jesus Life, live in me so that I may live in
  you.

Jesus Life, do not ever permit anything to
  separate me from you.

Jesus Life, grant that I may live eternally in
  the joy of your love.

Jesus Truth, may you shine in the world
  through me.

Jesus Way, may I be a faithful mirror of your
  example for others.

Jesus Life, may I be a channel of your grace
  and consolation to others.

Give Me All the Lonely People
By Chiara Lubich

Lord, give me all the lonely people.... My
heart has felt the passionate desire which
invades yours over the abandoned state in
which the whole world is afloat.

I feel love for each one who is sick and alone.

Whom do they have to comfort their tears?
Who shows compassion for them in their
  slow death?
Who hugs to their own heart the heart
  in despair?

O my God, grant that I may be in the world a
tangible sacrament of your love; let me be your
arms, hugging to myself all the loneliness in
the world and consuming it with love.

———————

To Fulfill My Mission
By Venerable John Henry Newman

O my God, I will put myself without reserve
into your hands.

God has created me to do him some defi-
nite service; he has committed some work to
me which he has not committed to another. I
have my mission—I may never know it in this
life, but I shall be told it in the next.

Somehow I am necessary for his purposes,
as necessary in my place as the archangel is in
his. If, indeed, I fail, he can raise another, as
he could make the stones the children of
Abraham. Yet I have a part in this great work.

I am a link in the chain, a bond of connection between persons. He has not created me for nothing. I shall do good, I shall do his work. I shall be an angel of peace, a preacher of truth in my own place, while not intending it, if I do but keep his commandments and serve him in my calling.

Therefore, I will trust him, whatever, wherever I am, I can never be thrown away. If I am in sickness, my sickness may serve Jesus; in perplexity, my perplexity may serve him; if I am in sorrow, my sorrow may serve him. My sickness, or perplexity, or sorrow may be necessary causes of some great end, which is quite beyond us.

He does nothing in vain. He may prolong my life, he may shorten it. He knows what he is about. He may take away my friends, he may throw me among strangers, he may make me feel desolate, make my spirits sink, hide the future from me—still he knows what he is about.

O Adonai...I give myself to you. I trust you wholly. You are wiser than I—more loving to me than I myself. Deign to fulfill your high purposes in me, whatever they may be—work in and through me. I am born to serve you; to be yours, to be your instrument. I ask not to see—I ask not to know—I ask simply to be used.

Complete your work, O Lord, and as you have loved me from the beginning, so make me love you to the end.

———————

Make Me an Instrument of Your Peace
By Saint Francis of Assisi

Lord, make me an instrument of your peace:
where there is hatred, let me sow love;
where there is discord, unity;
where there is injury, pardon;
where there is error, truth;
where there is doubt, faith;
where there is despair, hope;
where there is darkness, light;
where there is sadness, joy.

Divine Master,
grant that I may not so much seek
to be consoled as to console;
to be understood, as to understand;
to be loved, as to love.

For it is in giving that we receive;
it is in forgetting self that we find ourselves;
it is in pardoning that we are pardoned;
and it is in dying that we are born to
   eternal life.

———

For Love and Self-Surrender
By Saint Katharine Drexel

O give me, dear Mother Mary and Joseph, your love for Jesus, the depth of its tenderness. Grant me the grace of surrendering myself in all that shall happen to me today and in the future, to the mercy of God. God is all and at his summons everything must give way, even joy and happiness, which counts for nothing when he calls. If he calls to sorrow, he knows what is best, since faith and love feel real happiness by following where he leads.

As bread is changed into Jesus Christ, so must I be changed into Jesus Christ so that he alone will live in me.

———

Serenity Prayer
By Reinhold Niebuhr

God grant me the serenity
to accept the things I cannot change,
the courage to change the things I can,
and the wisdom to know the difference.

——— —

Lord Jesus, Rabbi, Teacher
By Kate Compston

Lord Jesus, Rabbi, Teacher,
thank you for reminding us
that until we bring you our darkness
  we cannot know your light;
that until we become servants of truth
  we cannot become wise leaders;
that until we are good listeners
  we cannot speak with authority;
that until we become willing, lifelong learners
  we cannot teach with insight or
  enthusiasm;
that until we are ready to be reborn
  we cannot truly mature.

Nourishing Our Lives
Prayers from the Hearts of Believers

∽∼∾

Tell Jesus everything.
If you have some troubles,
if your heart is full of hope...
confide even those worries that
you dare not say to anyone.
Tell Jesus everything.

—*Blessed James Alberione*

Transform Us, O Lord
Prayer for Someone Who Is Sick

Lord, my friend is sick
and has been this way for too long.
There is nothing I can do except
pray with my friend, asking together
    for healing.
Give us patience to see this through.
Help us look to your cross,
and to discern your suffering in our own.
Let the time spent in your Eucharistic
    presence
permeate and transform us both.
May this illness be a movement from
    suffering to joy,
a joy that has its source in you. Amen.

———

Refresh Me, O Lord
Prayer of a Caregiver

Here I am, Lord, kneeling in front of
   your tabernacle.
Give me the strength to keep caring.
Let me give others your love and
   compassion—
that love and compassion you gave so freely
   while on earth
to those who needed you.
I sometimes feel like my energy is
   ebbing away....
Where will I be refreshed, if not here
   with you?
Lord, the pain that I see every day,
   and my desire to help
brings me into your Eucharistic presence
to find my courage for one more day
of mirroring your faithful love. Amen.

———

Together We Mirror Your Love
Prayer Before Marriage

Lord God,
thank you for giving me my dearest love,
the one you have chosen for me,
the delight of my eyes that will never
   grow dim,
the one who will share the hours, days,
   and years with me.
May we love you by loving each other.
May we always do our best
for one another and our family,
making the ground we stand upon a
   holier place.
Let the Sacred Bread and Wine that we share
always be the Bread and Wine you give
   to us...
your Body and Blood that makes us holy.
And when there are shadows before us, Lord,
may we see the brighter light in you. Amen.

All Will Be Well with You
Facing a Difficult Decision

O God, would I love to get up from this
    kitchen table
and shift into a different gear.
This decision weighs upon me like a rock.
Help me to accept that
everything's in your hands.
Lord, it's all yours.
Then perhaps I'll be able to cry—
    salt takes away bitterness;
and smile, too—a sweetness for my soul.
And I'll sleep. Yes, a peaceful sleep...
the rest of someone secure in God's love.
Then I'll rise tomorrow morning
to meet you in the Bread of Life and Cup
    of Blessing.
And know that, with you, all will be well.
    Amen.

I Believe in Your Steadfast Love
Prayer For Special Needs

Jesus,
present in a special way in the Eucharist,
I come to talk with you about a special need.
Like Solomon who asked for wisdom,
and received everything else besides,
I, too, ask for your abundant blessings.

Lord, I desire wisdom and compassion,
and in particular, I confide to you my
   special need:
(here, mention your need).

I trust in your assurance that not even
   a sparrow
falls to the ground without your Father's
   knowledge.
Therefore, I wait upon your mercy,
for I believe that you will answer me. Amen.

Gift Us with Creative Love
Prayer To Have a Child

Lord,
we've prayed so long to have a child.
But it seems like time passes so quickly
and our hopes grow more fragile—
as fragile as the beginning of life,
as a feather on the wind of God.

Lord,
give us a joy with powerful energy
that bursts forth from our two lives
into another
in that beautiful exchange of creative love.
Let us know the wonders of having a child.
  Amen.

Thank You for This Child
Prayer of Thanks for Pregnancy

Lord Jesus,
I know what your Mother must have felt
when you were growing inside her.
Soft movements that are like so many mes-
 sages to my heart alone,
a new song that only my ears can perceive,
Love that brightens my heart.
Thank you, Lord, for this child,
this precious message, this lovely song,
this warm life that I have within me.
Your Body and Blood were fashioned in the
 same way.
The gift of yourself grew into the moment
 of Christmas,
and offers itself still in every Eucharist.
I feel as though I'm waiting for Christmas
 these nine months.
Help me to be the mother you are calling me
 to be. Amen.

Be the Food To Make Me Strong
Prayer for Recovery from Addiction

How much time has passed since I really
   felt free?
My shackles seem locked tight and I can
   think of nothing but the endless days and
   nights before me.
When will peace return?
Looking in a mirror, I weep to see myself old
   and worn.
"Once more, then I'll stop. Once again and
   no more..."
But today
I met you unexpectedly, God. I can't say why,
but I felt your presence.
Lord, you are the only one who can heal me.
You can break my shackles of addiction;
I'm too weak to break them myself.
Show me your power, mercy, and tenderness.
Forgive my craziness and uncertainty.
Be the Food that will make me strong enough
to say "No" and walk away.
Let me look at you with the clear eyes of
   new-found faith, and believe in a new day
   dawning. Amen.

Nourish Our Hope, Lord
Prayer after Miscarriage

Lord,
friends said depression would come and go,
   but now
this darkness seems so deep I wonder
   if I will ever
climb out and go on with my life.
My husband feels the same way, Lord.
We were so eager for this child.
But now she is a precious memory
for our hearts to embrace,
having entered your embrace forever.
Help us get through this darkness
and to know that, somehow, joy will
   come again.
Perhaps this is the key I'm looking for:
Hope is the heart's guiding light, and is
   nourished at the table
   of your Body.
Grant us that nourishment today. Amen.

Reveal Your Call, Lord
Prayer When Discerning a Religious Vocation

Father in heaven, I feel your grace tugging
   at me,
offering me a gift
that others don't seem to understand.
Do you want me to set my sails upon
the deep seas of your unfathomable call?
Will you give me power to cast
   the net of your Son's Gospel?
The strength to draw in his catch of
   humanity?
Jesus, you said of your redemptive work:
"I will draw all to myself."
When I encounter you in the Eucharist,
   Jesus,
my heart feels that familiar attraction.
If you are calling me, Lord, give me the grace
   to answer. Amen.

———————

Reach Out Through Me, O Lord
Prayer for a Loved One Away from Church

Well, Lord, love might be called an
openness of heart, but I feel so disheartened
that someone I love
doesn't feel the need to go to church.
Please, God, help me to see and appreciate
your goodness in those I live with—
even when we don't agree.
Let me feel heartened by knowing
that you can bring about the best
    from everything...
beyond my greatest hopes and desires.
When I receive your sacred Body and Blood
let me return home with you in my heart
so my dear ones will feel you near
and open their own hearts to your presence
    in me. Amen.

I Hunger, O Lord
Prayer After the Death of a Child

Lord, it happened so quickly. I scarcely
took my eyes from my child and death,
like a thief,
snatched my little one away.
One moment sleeping in my arms,
the next moment in your arms, not mine.
My tears flow unceasingly and
my anger with you flares unexpectedly.
Lord, give me the grace to get through
   this storm.
Help me to live through my sorrow and sort
   through the blame.
I hunger for my child with hunger pangs that
   cut so deeply:
Feed me with your Body and Blood,
   the promise
that we will be together again, the promise
of eternal life. Amen.

Have Mercy on the Grieving
Prayer When a Parent Dies

Time passes so quickly.
Just yesterday I was a child.
Now an adult, I suddenly feel so alone in
   this world.
I am worried about decisions I will have
   to make
now that I have no one to rely on for advice.
O Bread of our Living, Life for the world,
be near me as I struggle through this time
   of sorrow.
I entrust my parent and myself to your care.
Lord Jesus, Lamb of God, you take away
the sin of the world. Have mercy on me and
   on all who grieve. Amen.

———————

Grasp My Hand and Pull Me Up
Prayer on the Loss of Employment

Lord, this is a fine mess! What am I going to
do without a job?
Who will pay the bills, how are we going
to eat?
What about the mortgage and the doctor visits?
I can't believe this has happened!
I've heard it said that, "We don't shape God;
God shapes us."
Are you telling me you have something better
in store?
Help me to be patient and not mistrust you.
I want to believe that you will grasp my hand
and pull me up from the waters I am
sinking in.
Then, like you and Peter in the storm, we will
walk to the boat together.
On the shore, we will break the Bread
and drink the Wine that you alone know
how to pour.
And I will know the deep joy of total surren-
der to you. Amen.

Give Me the Peace That Comes From You
Prayer for Dealing with Past Abuse

Dear Lord,
a thousand times I have told myself: "I need
 to face the past."
And a thousand times I have turned my back
 in fear.
But now, O God, source of all truth and
 holy desires,
I feel ready to begin searching my heart,
because you are at my side.
Hide me under your wings and protect me.
Rescue me from the fears that may come;
give me the peace the world cannot give.
Feed me on this journey, O Bread of Light
 and Truth,
O Food of Travelers and Strength of
 the Weary.
Be glad in the Lord, my heart, and shine like
 a star
in the darkness of the night. Amen.

Help Me to Keep Believing
Prayer for a Loved One in Dangerous Circumstances

Jesus, I feel such anxiety, knowing that those
I love are facing danger.
Faintly, I hear you say, "My grace is sufficient
for you;
my strength is made perfect in your
weakness."
And still I plead for their safety: be with
them and protect them.
Bolster my hope with a boldness that refuses
to be discouraged;
give patience to my faith so I may trust in
you.
I call upon you, Jesus, given as our food in
the Sacred Feast.
Let me hear you say,
"I want to fill you—pressed down and overflowing—with my richness.
I am greater than all danger."
Help me to keep believing. Amen.

You Are the Resurrection
Prayer Upon Diagnosis

The tests came back. I only heard
one word and my insides began quivering.
Terminal. No hope for healing.
My eyes blurred with tears I couldn't
    keep back.
Where are you, Jesus? Why didn't I feel you
    there with me?
Why can't I feel you now? Are you in
    my heart?
I'm so scared.
Help me to remember that through it all
you are the Resurrection and the Life.
"I am the Bread of Life. You who come to me
    shall not hunger.
If you believe in me, you shall live forever."
May I penetrate the mystery of your dying
    and your rising
and trust in your ever-present love. Amen.

Nourish and Comfort Me, Jesus
Prayer When a Friend Betrays

Lord, my dearest Friend
who never abandons me, never disappoints
   his friends,
a very good friend of mine has betrayed me.
I trusted,
and now wish I had been discreet.
If truth is the basis of friendship,
right now I have only you.
You call us your friends.
You confide to us the mystery of your
   own pain.
You share with us your Body and Blood.
You, too, suffered a friend's betrayal—
and you still suffer betrayal today.
Lord Jesus, be with me in the gift of yourself
in the Eucharistic Bread and Wine,
and give my heart strength in this moment
   of confusion.
Nourish and comfort me, Jesus. Amen.

Offer Peace to Every Heart
Prayer After Someone's Suicide

Lord Jesus,
Bread of Life and Wine of Promise,
break through this horror with some kind
  of understanding,
some light for the pitiful darkness in
  my heart.
Give me a deeper form of seeing, Lord.
Lift my eyes from the chaos of this world,
from the brokenness I feel before this death.
Lord, stay with us who remain in this world.
And I pray: dismiss your poor servant with a
  blessing, Lord,
and forgive all that has taken place.
Fill us with courage through your Body,
given *for* us and *to* us. Impart peace in every
  heart. Amen.

Be Bread for Our Journey

Prayer in Financial Crisis

They say any concern too small to be turned
    into a prayer is
too small to be turned into a burden.
Well, Lord, poor and patient, here is
    my burden...
and it doesn't feel small:
I am in a financial crunch.
I don't know how I will make ends meet.
I place all my trust in you, because
    you walked
the land with hardly anything to live on.
So I'll make this request short, Lord:
    I'm broke.
Help me to do what I can
with the best that I have to turn this
    situation around.
Just see me through this time.
Give me the trust flowing from your
    Eucharistic presence.
Be Bread for my journey. Amen.

We Meet Each Other in You
Prayer When a Spouse Dies

Lord God,
my loved one is gone.
No amount
of ardor, anger, grief, or anguish
can bring my spouse back.
I can only hope to hallow our memories
and ask you to lessen the loneliness I feel
when thoughts of the one I've spent my
   life with
assail and overwhelm my heart.
Bless me, Lord, with clear vision
so I may keep my eyes fixed on you.
Surround me not only with your light,
but with the light of my loved one who is
   in your light.
I yearn to receive your Body and Blood with
   deeper love than ever before
knowing that my spouse remains in your
   Mystical Body
and we can still meet in you. Amen.

You Are the Center of Our Lives
Prayer of Thanksgiving for God's Gift of Eucharist

Thank you, Lord Jesus, for being the center of
   our lives.
The gift of your holy presence in the
   Eucharist,
given *for* us and given *to* us,
can bring us peace and contentment
despite problems that often oppress.
I believe that in the depths of my soul
you and the Father and the Spirit are one.
May I plumb the depths of your love
every time I participate in the Eucharist
and receive your Body and Blood.
May I empty myself of everything
in order to be filled with you,
who offer yourself every day for the life of
   the world. Amen.

Interceding for the World
Prayers for Particular Needs

〜〜〜

Be "big~hearted" enough in
prayer to embrace everyone
in the world.

—*Venerable Mother Thecla Merlo*

Prayer of Blessing Upon the World
Psalm 67:1–5

May God be gracious to us and bless us
　　and make his face to shine upon us,
that your way may be known upon earth,
　　your saving power among all nations.
Let the peoples praise you, O God;
　　let all the peoples praise you.

Let the nations be glad and sing for joy,
　　for you judge the peoples with equity
　　and guide the nations upon earth.
Let the peoples praise you, O God;
　　let all the peoples praise you.

———— ————

The Heart of All Hearts
By Chiara Lubich

For me to talk about you, Jesus, in
　　the Eucharist
is really quite daring and presumptuous.

For you are present in all the churches of
the world,
listening to the intimate secrets, the hidden
problems,
and the sighs of millions of people,
seeing the tears of joy in the conversions you
alone know about.
You are the heart of all hearts, the heart of
the Church.
We would prefer not to disturb the silence
which is fitting for such a sublime and
breathtaking love
except that our own love, eager to overcome
every fear,
desires to go beyond the veils of the white
host and the wine in the golden chalice.
Forgive our daring:
for love wants to know better in order to
love better.
We do not want our journey on earth to
be over
before we have discovered at least a little
about who you are.

Prayer for Unity
By Basil Hume

Lord Jesus Christ,
you said
may they all be one, just as, Father,
you are in me and I am in you,
so that the world may believe
it was you who sent me.
Dear Lord, bring together in love and peace
all who believe in you. Amen.

God of Love
By Saint Teresa of Avila

God of love, help us to remember
that Christ has no body now on earth
  but ours,
no hands but ours, no feet but ours.
Ours are the eyes to see the needs of
  the world.
Ours are the hands with which to bless
  everyone now.
Ours are the feet with which he is to go
  about doing good.

Give Us Courage
By Women of Brazil

Blessed Lord, you who know each one of our fears, release us from them all by your love and give us courage to act:

—against rejection, and for your love;

—against oppression, and for justice;

—against poverty, and for life abundant;

—against sickness, and for wholeness;

—against loneliness, and for companionship;

—against violence, and for peace;

—against death, and for life.

———— ————

Embrace the Whole World
By Saint Faustina Kowalska

O living Host, my one and only Strength, Fountain of love and mercy, embrace the whole world, fortify those who are weak! (*Diary*, 223)

———— ————

Prayer for the Oppressed
Psalm 17:1–13, 15

Hear a just cause, O LORD; attend to my cry;
  give ear to my prayer from lips free of
      deceit.
From you let my vindication come;
  let your eyes see the right.

If you try my heart, if you visit me by night,
  if you test me, you will find no
      wickedness in me;
  my mouth does not transgress.
As for what others do, by the word of
      your lips
  I have avoided the ways of the violent.
My steps have held fast to your paths;
  my feet have not slipped.

I call upon you, for you will answer me,
      O God;
  incline your ear to me, hear my words.
Wondrously show your steadfast love,
  O savior of those who seek refuge
  from their adversaries at your right hand.

Guard me as the apple of the eye;
  hide me in the shadow of your wings,

from the wicked who despoil me,
  my deadly enemies who surround me.
They close their hearts to pity;
  with their mouths they speak arrogantly.
They track me down; now they surround me;
  they set their eyes to cast me to the ground.
They are like a lion eager to tear,
  like a young lion lurking in ambush.

Rise up, O LORD, confront them,
      overthrow them!
As for me, I shall behold your face in
      righteousness;
  when I awake I shall be satisfied, beholding
      your likeness.

———————

A Center of Love
By Blessed Pope John XXIII

Every believer must be a spark of light, a center of love, a vivifying leaven amidst his or her
fellow human beings; and every believer will
be this all the more perfectly the more closely
he or she lives in communion with God.

———————

For the Needs of Others
By Saint Anselm

God of love, whose compassion never fails,
we bring you the sufferings of the world;
the needs of the homeless,
the cries of prisoners,
the pains of the sick and injured,
the sorrow of the bereaved,
the helplessness of the elderly and weak.
According to their needs and your great
   mercy,
strengthen and relieve them
in Jesus Christ our Lord.

Becoming One in Christ
By Ronald A. Knox

Lord God,
the whole notion of Christian solidarity
grows out of
and is centered in
the common participation of a common
   table.
As the many grains of wheat
are ground together into one loaf,

as the many grapes
are pressed together in one cup,
so we, being many, are one in Christ.
How could we be one *with* Christ,
without becoming one *in* Christ?

――― ―――

For Friends and Loved Ones
By Saint Gertrude the Great and Saint Mechtilde

Lord, I see clearly that any affection which I
have ever had is scarcely as one drop in the
vast ocean of all the seas, when compared
with the tenderness of thy divine heart to-
wards those whom I love.... Therefore, I cannot even by one thought wish anything other
than that which thy almighty wisdom has ap-
pointed for each of them.... Lord, bless thy
special friends and mine, according to the
good pleasure of thy divine goodness.

――― ―――

Intercessions
By David M. Turoldo

We pray untiringly, interceding for all our
   brothers and sisters, and we ask:
—*Lord, hear our prayer.*

O Father, you love us with a boundless love,
—break down our selfish barriers and transform us into a loving presence.

O Father, you are the origin of everything
   that exists and the goal toward which all
   creation tends,
—make us aware that our lives are marked
   by your seal and that you lead everything
   to your perfection.

Lord Jesus Christ, at times we grow weary of
   believing in the mystery of your complete
   humanity,
—confirm our weak faith and help us always
   to discover your face in the faces of our
   brothers and sisters.

Lord Jesus Christ, you are light for all who
   seek and accept you,

—enlighten our hearts, so we can follow you
along the path you trod in obedience to the
Father.

O Holy Spirit, final gift of the Son made
flesh, you dwell within us and lead us to
the kingdom,
—give us the strength to resist the
seductions of the evil one, so that we do
not obscure the light of your presence
within us.

O Holy Spirit, you urge us always toward
wider horizons in the mystery of the
encounter with God in time,
—enable us to recognize in every person a
brother or sister whom the Father loves
and for whom the Lord Jesus gave his life.

For the Troubled of the World
By Women of Sweden

We pray for those in the world who have for-
gotten that all people are made in your image
and likeness and are of equal worth in your
eyes; for those who suffer because of racial
oppression and social injustice; for those who
struggle for human dignity; for those who
have lost their hope for the future.

We pray for the needy and suffering
   in the world;
for the hungry and thirsty;
for the homeless;
for the unemployed;
for the victims of alcoholism;
for the victims of drug addiction;
for the sick, in mind or body;
for the lonely and the elderly.

We pray for all parents, that they may give
their children the love and guidance which
will help them to find the right way in life;
for all children without parents;

for young people, that they may find hope
   for the future;
for peace between nations and good will
   among all people;
Lord, hear us!

Prayer for Priests
Adapted from Pope John Paul II

Jesus, eternal High Priest,
bless all priests so that they may fulfill their
   priestly vocation:
to believe profoundly,
to profess their faith with courage,
to pray fervently,
to teach with deep conviction,
to serve,
to put into practice in their own lives
the program of the beatitudes,
to know how to love disinterestedly,
to be close to everyone,
especially those who are most in need.

Prayer for Awareness
By Joyce Rupp

Generous God, you smile upon the wide diversity and beauty in the humanity whom you have created, but you weep at the great divide between the rich and the poor. I come today with the taste of ego-centeredness on my spiritual breath. I beg to have greater awareness and a deeper commitment to what will heal my world. Help me to make good decisions about my daily living so that who I am and what I do can have a positive effect on my brothers and sisters everywhere on this vast planet.

Stretch my vision so that I do not forget those who hunger and search for shelter each day. Remind me when I am using and buying material things, to do so with care. Enable me to use the earth's resources responsibly so that there will be enough to go around for all who live on this green planet today and in the future.

Awaken me each day to gratitude for all that I so easily take for granted. Let my eyes do more than just read the stories in the daily paper or watch them on the evening news. Let my eyes take those stories to my heart where I am one with all who dwell on the earth. Touch my compassion so that I know the pain of the hungry, the violated, the homeless, the burdened, and all those who yearn for some of my riches.

Compassionate Creator, stir in my soul. Call to me again and again, to be a true child of the universe. May I be attentive and alert to how you would have me live my abundant life. Grant me the generosity to share it with others.

———————

To Foster Respect for Life
By Pope John Paul II

O Mary,
bright dawn of the new world,
Mother of the living,
to you do we entrust the cause of life:
Look down, O Mother,
upon the vast numbers
of babies not allowed to be born,
of the poor whose lives are made difficult,
of men and women who are victims of brutal
    violence,
of the elderly and the sick killed
by indifference or out of misguided mercy.
Grant that all who believe in your Son
may proclaim the Gospel of life
with honesty and love
to the people of our time.
Obtain for them the grace
to accept that Gospel
as a gift ever new,
the joy of celebrating it with gratitude
throughout their lives,
and the courage to bear witness to it
resolutely, in order to build,
together with all people of good will,

the civilization of truth and love,
to the praise and glory of God,
the Creator and lover of life.

——————

Prayer for Ministers of the Word
By Blessed James Alberione

O Mary, you who gave birth to the Word
  made flesh, be present among us: assist,
  inspire, and comfort the ministers of the
  Word.
O Mary, you who are Queen of the Apostles,
  intervene with your protection that the
  light of the Gospel may reach all peoples.
O Mary, Mother of Jesus, Way, Truth, and
  Life, intercede for us, so that heaven may
  be filled with those who sing the hymn of
  glory to the most Holy Trinity.

——————

For a World Freed from Consumerism
Psalm 49:1–12, 16–19

Hear this, all you peoples;
  give ear, all inhabitants of the world,
both low and high,
  rich and poor together.
My mouth shall speak wisdom;
  the meditation of my heart shall be
      understanding.
I will incline my ear to a proverb;
  I will solve my riddle to the music of
      the harp.

Why should I fear in times of trouble,
  when the iniquity of my persecutors
      surrounds me,
those who trust in their wealth
  and boast of the abundance of their riches?
Truly, no ransom avails for one's life,
  there is no price one can give to God for it.
For the ransom of life is costly,
  and can never suffice
that one should live on forever
  and never see the grave.

When we look at the wise, they die;
  fool and dolt perish together
  and leave their wealth to others.
Their graves are their homes forever,
  their dwelling places to all generations,
  though they named lands their own.
Mortals cannot abide in their pomp;
  they are like the animals that perish.

Do not be afraid when some become rich,
  when the wealth of their houses increases.
For when they die they will carry
      nothing away;
  their wealth will not go down after them.
Though in their lifetime they count
      themselves happy
  —for you are praised when you do well
      for yourself—
they will go to the company of their ancestors,
  who will never again see the light.

————

Prayer for Vocations
By Pope John Paul II

Mary, your life was a humble and generous service. You were servant of the Word when the angel announced to you the divine plan of salvation. You were servant of the Son, giving him life and remaining open to his mystery.

You were servant of redemption, standing courageously at the foot of the cross, close to the Suffering Servant and Lamb, who was sacrificing himself for love of us. You were servant of the Church on the day of Pentecost, and with your intercession you continue to generate her in every believer, even in these our difficult and troubled times.

Let the young people of the third millennium look to you, young daughter of Israel, who have known the agitation of a young heart when faced with the plan of the eternal God. Make them able to accept the invitation of your Son to give their lives wholly for the glory of God.

Make them understand that to serve God satisfies the heart, and that only in the service of God and of his kingdom do we realize ourselves in accordance with the divine plan, and life becomes a hymn of glory to the most Holy Trinity. Amen.

Favorite Eucharistic Hymns

～～

Sing to the LORD, bless his
name;
tell of his salvation
from day to day.

—*Psalm 96:2*

Alleluia! Bread of Angels
By William C. Dix

Alleluia! Bread of angels,
here on earth our food, our stay!
Alleluia! here the sinful
flee to you from day to day:
Intercessor, friend of sinners,
earth's redeemer, plead for me,
where the songs of all the sinless
sweep across the crystal sea.

Alleluia! King Eternal,
you the Lord of Lords we own.
Alleluia! Born of Mary,
earth thy footstool,
heaven thy throne.
You within the veil have entered
robed in flesh, our great High Priest.
You on earth, both priest and victim
In the Eucharistic feast.

Let All Mortal Flesh Keep Silent
Traditional

Let all mortal flesh keep silent,
and with fear and trembling stand;

ponder nothing earthly-minded,
for with blessing in his hand,
Christ our God to earth descendeth,
our full homage to demand.

King of kings, yet born of Mary,
as of old on earth he stood,
Lord of Lords, in human vesture,
in the Body and the Blood.
He will give to all the faithful
his own self for heavenly food.

Rank on rank the host of heaven
spreads its vanguard on the way,
as the Light of lights descendeth
from the realms of endless day
that the powers of hell may vanish
as the darkness clears away.

At his feet the six winged seraph,
cherubim with sleepless eye,
veil their faces to the presence,
as with ceaseless voice they cry,
"alleluia, alleluia,
alleluia, Lord Most High!"

Adoramus Te
Traditional

Adoramus Te, Christe, et benedicimus Tibi,
Adoramus Te, Christe, et benedicimus Tibi,
Quia per sanctam crucem Tuam redemisti
  mundum.
Adoramus Te, Christe, et benedicimus Tibi.
Adoramus Te, Christe.

Panis Angelicus
Traditional

Panis Angélicus fit panis homínum.
Dat panis cáelicus figúris términum:
O res mirábilis! Mandúcat Dóminum
Pauper, servus, et húmilis.

Te trina Déitas únaque póscimus.
Sic nos tu vísita, sicut te cólimus;
Per tuas sémitas duc nos quo téndimus,
Ad lucem quam inhábitas. Amen.

O Saving Victim, Opening Wide
(O Salutaris Hostia)
Traditional

O Saving Victim, opening wide
The gate of heav'n to man below!
Our foes press on from ev'ry side:
Thine aid supply, Thy strength bestow.

To Thy great name be endless praise,
Immortal Godhead, one in three;
Oh, grant us endless length of days
In our true native land with Thee. Amen.

O salutáris Hóstia
Quae caeli pandis óstium.
Bella premunt hostília,
Da robur, fer auxílium.

Uni trinóque Domino
Sit sempitérna glória.
Qui vitam sine término
Nobis donet in pátria. Amen.

Humbly Let Us Voice Our Homage
(Tantum Ergo Sacramentum)
By Saint Thomas Aquinas

Humbly let us voice our homage
for so great a Sacrament;
let all former rites surrender
to the Lord's New Testament;
what our senses fail to fathom
let us grasp through faith's consent.

Glory, honor, adoration,
let us sing with one accord.
Praised be God almighty Father;
praised be Christ, his Son, our Lord;
praised be God the Holy Spirit;
Triune Godhead be adored. Amen.

Tantum ergo Sacraméntum
venerémur cérnui;
et antíquum documéntum,
novo cedat rítui;
praestet fides suppleméntum,
sénsuum deféctui.

Genitóri, genitóque
laus et jubilátio,
salus, honor, virtus quoque

sit et benedíctio:
procedénti ab utróque
compar sit laudátio. Amen.

———

Sweet Sacrament
By Father Fredrick Faber

Jesus! My Lord, my God, my all!
How can I love thee as I ought?
And how revere this wondrous gift,
So far surpassing hope or thought?

Chorus:
  Sweet Sacrament! We thee adore!
  O make us love thee more and more!

Had I but Mary's sinless heart
To love thee with, my dearest King!
Oh, with what bursts of fervent praise
Thy goodness, Jesus, would I sing! *Chorus.*

Oh! See upon the altar placed
The Victim of divinest love!
Let all the earth below adore,
And join the choirs of heav'n above. *Chorus.*

———

The Divine Praises
Traditional

Blessed be God.

Blessed be his Holy Name.

Blessed be Jesus Christ, true God and
true Man.

Blessed be the name of Jesus.

Blessed be his most Sacred Heart.

Blessed be his most Precious Blood.

Blessed be Jesus in the most holy Sacrament
of the Altar.

Blessed be the Holy Spirit the Paraclete.

Blessed be the great Mother of God, Mary
most holy.

Blessed be her holy and Immaculate
Conception.

Blessed be her glorious Assumption.

Blessed be the name of Mary, Virgin
and Mother.

Blessed be Saint Joseph, her most chaste
spouse.

Blessed be God in his angels and in his
saints.

Hail, True Body
Ascribed to Innocent VI

Hail, true Body of the Savior,
Spotless Mary's virgin birth!
Slain upon the cross to cleanse us
By His pains from sins of earth.

Chorus:
  Hear us, merciful and gracious,
  O sweet Jesus, Mary's Child.

From whose side for sinners piercéd,
Water flow'd and mingled blood,
May'st thou, dearest Lord, be given
In death's hour to be our food. *Chorus.*

Lord, in loving contemplation
Fix our hearts and eyes on thee,
Till we taste thy full salvation,
And thine unveiled glories see. *Chorus.*

Honor, glory, virtue, merit,
Be to thee, O Virgin's Son!
With the Father, and the Spirit,
While eternal ages run. *Chorus.*

Pange Lingua
By Saint Thomas Aquinas

Sing my tongue the Savior's glory,
of his flesh the mystery sing;
of the Blood all price exceeding
shed by our immortal King,
destined for the world's redemption
from a noble womb to spring.

Of a pure and spotless virgin
born for us on earth below,
he, as man with man conversing,
stayed the seeds of truth to sow;
then he closed in solemn order
wondrously his life of woe.

On the night of that last supper,
seated with his chosen band,
he the Paschal Victim eating,
first fulfills the law's command;
then as food to his apostles,
gives himself with his own hand.

Word made flesh, the bread of nature
by his word to flesh he turns;
wine into his blood he changes—

what though sense no change discerns?
Only be the heart in earnest,
faith her lesson quickly learns. Amen.

———

Jesus, Food of Angels
By Saint Alphonsus Liguori

Jesus, food of angels,
Monarch of the heart;
Oh, that I could never
From thy face depart!
Yes, thou ever dwellest
Here for love of me,
Hidden thou remainest
God of majesty.

Soon I hope to see thee,
And enjoy thy love,
Face to face, sweet Jesus,
In thy heav'n above.
But on earth an exile,
My delight shall be
Ever to be near thee
Veil'd for love of me.

———

At the Lamb's High Feast We Sing
Traditional

At the Lamb's high feast we sing,
Praise to our victorious King,
Who hath washed us in the tide
Flowing from his piercéd side;
Praise we him, whose love divine
Gives his sacred blood for wine,
Gives his body for the feast,
Christ the Victim, Christ the Priest.

Where the Paschal blood is poured,
Death's dark angel sheathes his sword;
Israel's hosts triumphant go
Through the wave that drowns the foe.
Praise we Christ, whose blood was shed,
Paschal Victim, paschal Bread;
With sincerity and love
Eat we Manna from above.

Mighty Victim from the sky,
Hell's fierce powers beneath thee lie;
Thou hast conquered in the fight,
Thou hast brought us life and light;
Now no more can death appall,
Now no more the grave enthrall;
Thou hast opened Paradise,
And in thee thy saints shall rise.

Paschal triumph, Easter joy,
Only sin can this destroy;
From sin's death do thou set free
Souls reborn, O Lord, in thee.
Hymns of glory and of praise,
Father, to thee we raise;
Risen Lord, all praise to thee,
Ever with the Spirit be.

O God of Loveliness
By Saint Alphonsus Liguori

O God of loveliness,
O Lord of heav'n above,
How worthy to possess
My heart's devoted love.
So sweet your countenance,
So gracious to behold,
That one, one only glance were bliss untold.

You are blest three in one,
Yet undivided still;
You are that One alone
Whose love my heart can fill.
The heav'ns and earth below
Were fashioned by Your word;
How great, how great you are, O holy Lord!

O Loveliness supreme,
And Beauty infinite!
O everflowing stream
And ocean of delight!
O Life by which I live,
My truest Life above,
I give you, Lord, my undivided love.

Be Thou My Vision
Ancient Gaelic Hymn

Be thou my vision, O Lord of my heart;
Naught is all else to me save that thou art.
Thou my best thought by day and by night;
Waking or sleeping, thy presence my Light.

Be thou my wisdom, thou my true Word;
I ever with thee, thou with me Lord.
Thou my great Father, I thy dear son;
Thou in me dwelling, I with thee one.

Be thou my battleshield, sword for the fight.
Be thou my dignity, thou my delight.
Thou my soul's shelter, thou my high tow'r;
Raise thou me heavenward, Pow'r of my
    pow'r.

Riches I need not nor man's empty praise,
Thou my inheritance now and always.
Thou and thou only, first in my heart,
High King of heaven, my treasure thou art.

Heart of my own heart whatever befall,
Still be my vision, O Ruler of all.
Be thou my vision, O Lord of my heart.
Naught is all else to me save that thou art.

Godhead Here in Hiding
Ascribed to Saint Thomas Aquinas

Godhead here in hiding, whom I do adore
Masked by these bare shadows, shape and
    nothing more,
See, Lord, at thy service low lies here a heart
Lost, all lost in wonder at the God Thou art.

On the cross thy Godhead made no sign
    to men;
Here thy very manhood steals from
    human ken;
Both are my confession, both are my belief,
And I pray the pray'r of the dying thief.

I am not like Thomas, wounds I cannot see,
But I plainly call thee Lord and God as he;
This faith each day deeper be my holding of,
Daily make me harder hope and dearer love.

Jesus, whom I look at shrouded here below,
I beseech thee send me what I long for so,
Some day to gaze on thee face to face in light
And be blest for ever with thy glory's sight.

Spirit Seeking Light and Beauty
By Janet Stuart

Spirit seeking light and beauty,
Heart that longest for thy rest.
Soul that asketh understanding,
Only thus can ye be blest.
Through the vastness of creation,
Though your restless thought may roam,
God is all that you can long for,
God is all his creatures' home.

Taste and see him, feel and hear him,
Hope and grasp his unseen hand;
Though the darkness seem to hide him,
Faith and love can understand.
God, who lovest all thy creatures,
All our hearts are known to thee;
Lead us through the land of shadows
To thy blest eternity.

Hours of Adoration

❧❧❧

From this vital source,
the Eucharistic Master,
everything is given life.

—*Blessed James Alberione*

How to Make an Hour of Adoration

Blessed James Alberione (1884–1971), the Founder of the Pauline Family, was an Italian priest who daily celebrated the Eucharist and spent four to five hours in adoration and contemplation of the Word of God. The Eucharist became the focal point of his day, sustaining an immensely hectic and active apostolic lifestyle. Blessed Alberione developed a special Christ-centered way of making an hour of adoration that is scripturally-based, flexible, and easy to use.

While there are many ways of making an hour of adoration, we offer here the Pauline method developed by Blessed James Alberione. It is a way of adoring Jesus in the Eucharist that responds to our yearnings for healing and fulfillment, and which allows not only for personal transformation, but also the transformation of the society in which we live.

At the heart of Blessed Alberione's Eucharistic spirituality is Jesus, who is our Way, Truth, and Life. Jesus not only proclaims the truth, but is himself our Truth because it is in him that we discover the loving face of God. Jesus shows us the Way to the Father by the example he gave in living among us, but also by walking with us on our journey. As our Life, Jesus saves us from the darkness of sin and invites us to the deepest possible fulfillment by sharing in the mystery of his life, death, and resurrection. When we enter more deeply into relationship with Jesus, Way, Truth, and Life, we discover that our daily life begins to change and grow. Our relationship with the Lord begins to impact our relationship with others and with the world itself, paving the way for an increase of justice, peace, and responsibility for others as our neighbors.

The hour of adoration is divided into three "moments," or parts, based on the threefold definition Jesus gave of himself as Way, Truth, and Life. A rigid time division of this hour is not important, however; what is essential is that time be given to each of these three moments.

Adoring Jesus Truth

In the first part, we adore Jesus, listening attentively to his Word to us today and letting his truth shape our minds and attitudes.

At the beginning of the hour of adoration (or beforehand), we can choose a theme for the hour, or recall a particular need or grace we want to keep before us in prayer. We begin with a hymn or prayer of adoration.

Then, asking the light of the Holy Spirit, we read a passage of Scripture, chosen according to the theme, and adore Jesus in his Word. We are attentive to the Word, not only with our ears, but also with our hearts, letting Jesus Truth enlighten us and give us new understanding and insight. We can reread the Scripture passage, or converse with Jesus about how it touches our life and what it means for us today, in our situation. The reading may be long or short. What is important is to leave time for reflection, allowing

Jesus' saving Word to enlighten us here and now. After about twenty minutes, we conclude by responding to the Word of God with an act of faith, an affirmation of our belief in and our commitment to Christ.

——— · ———

Following Jesus Way

Having just recommitted ourselves to Christ, we now turn to contemplate Jesus as our Way and our Model, and we look more closely at our relationship with him.

Taking up the theme of the Scripture passage and our reflection, we contemplate God's action in our own lives. First, we thank God for the many and marvelous ways we have been touched by God's loving gifts. As we become aware of God's many blessings, we realize that we have often failed to respond to those blessings. We then confront our lives with Jesus' words and example. We ask ourselves how Jesus is calling us to follow him more closely and how we need to change—in our attitudes, actions, or desires—so that we can become more like him. Then, we express

sorrow for our sinfulness and renew our resolve to more faithfully follow our loving
Master in the concrete way we live. We can
also renew our trust that God will give us the
graces we need to change. Jesus wants us to
trust in him so that we can be his presence in
the world today.

———

Sharing Jesus' Life

Converted anew, we try to open our
hearts completely to Jesus Life, to let his sustaining grace and peace touch our hearts so
that we can bring that same peace and love to
others.

In this third part, we unite ourselves to
Jesus Life, and contemplate his love for the
Father, for all humanity, and for each of us.
We bring to God our own needs and the
needs of the world. Prayer, in this third part,
can be offered spontaneously, spilling from
the fullness of our hearts, or it can take the
form of the Rosary, the Stations of the Cross,
the Liturgy of the Hours, a psalm, or other
prayers. This is time for "prayer of the heart,"

that is, letting ourselves be loved by the Lord, sharing with God our needs and our deepest desires, and asking to be transformed into witnesses of his love and truth.

We conclude our hour of adoration with an act of love and return to daily life not only refreshed and renewed, but more aware of our call to bring the fullness of our life in Christ to the world in which we live and work.

Jesus, Our Way, Truth, and Life

಍ೲ

Theme

To let my life be transformed in Christ

Introduction

During the Last Supper, Jesus spoke from his heart to his disciples. Take a few moments to adore Jesus who died and rose for you, who wants so much to be part of your life that he nourishes you in Communion, who wants so much to be close to you that he remains present here in the Eucharist in silence and simplicity.

∽

Adoring Jesus Truth

I ask the Holy Spirit, whom Jesus gave to us as our "Intercessor" before the Father, to flood my soul with divine light, so that I will receive the Word of God fully into my heart, allowing his living Word to transform my perspective, my attitudes, my feelings, my life.

Reading
John 14:1–21[*]

"Let not your hearts be troubled!
Believe in God and believe in me.
In my Father's house are many rooms;
were it not so, would I have told you that I'm
   going to prepare a place for you?
And if I go and prepare a place for you,
I'll come again and take you to myself,
so that where I am, you, too, may be.
Yet where I'm going, you know the way."

Thomas said to him, "Lord, we don't know where you're going! How can we know the way?" Jesus said to him,
"I am the way and the truth and the life;
no one comes to the Father except through me.

If you know me you'll know the the Father, too,
and from now on you will know him and
   will see him.

Philip said to him, "Lord, show us the Father
and we'll be satisfied." Jesus said to him,

"Have I been with you so long and yet you
   don't recognize me, Philip?
Whoever has seen me has seen the Father!
How can you say, 'Show us the Father'?
Don't you believe that I am in the Father
   and the Father is in me?
The words I speak to you I do not speak on
   my own,
but the Father who abides in me does his
   works.
Believe *me* when I say that I am in the Father
and the Father is in me,
but if you don't, believe because of the works
   themselves.
Amen, amen, I say to you,
whoever believes in me,
   the works I do he, too, will do,
and he'll do greater works than these,
   because I'm going to the Father!

And whatever you ask for in my name, I'll do
    it, so the Father may be glorified in the Son;
if you ask me for anything in my name,
    I'll do it.

If you love me, you'll keep my
    commandments,
and I'll ask the Father and he'll give you
    another Intercessor to be with you forever,
the Spirit of truth, whom the world cannot
    accept because it doesn't see or know him.
You'll know him, because he will remain
    with you and be in you.
I won't leave you orphaned—I'll come
    to you.
In a little while the world will no longer see
    me, but *you'll* see me;
because *I* will live, you, too, will live.
On that day you'll realize that I am in my
    Father, and you in me and I in you.
Whoever keeps my commandments and
    obeys them—
he it is who loves me,
while whoever loves me is loved by my
    Father, and I'll love him and reveal myself
    to him."

Reflection

In this powerful yet consoling passage, Jesus invites you to enter more deeply into a personal relationship with him—a relationship that can encompass any pressure, any difficulty, any joy or trouble. Jesus wants you to experience the security of being loved faithfully, unconditionally: "Let not your hearts be troubled!"

The words, "I am the Way, the Truth, and the Life," are not only a profound self-definition and a description of Jesus' relationship with us. They are also a dazzling yet mysterious promise of loving fidelity and companionship. What might these words of Jesus mean to you?

In the Paschal Mystery, Jesus shows us our true value in God's eyes: the love of the Trinity poured out through Jesus for humanity, for the sake of each one of us. Jesus' self-sacrificing love revealed in the Eucharist becomes the foundation of our way of thinking, living, praying—the Truth which truly sets us free.

In his humble and self-forgetting Eucharistic presence, Jesus is our Way, our faithful Companion, and our Model for how to live in true freedom and obedience to the Father.

In transforming bread and wine into his own Body and Blood, Jesus nourishes us with his own life, literally becoming our Life and infusing comfort, strength, joy, and fruitfulness—both for ourselves and for those whose lives we touch.

Take a few minutes to reflect on your relationship with Jesus. How is Jesus *your* Way, *your* Truth, and *your* Life? How can you enter more deeply into relationship with Jesus?

As a response to the reading, renew your faith in Jesus:

Act of Faith in Jesus' Promises

Jesus, I believe you are the Word who became flesh and lived among us, offering us grace and truth.

Jesus, I believe you are the Lamb of God who takes away our sins.

Jesus, I believe you are the Master who invites us to discipleship, growth, humility, and an ever greater love.

Jesus, I believe you are God's beloved Son, sent into the world to save us.

Jesus, I believe you are Living Water, who
quenches our thirst for meaning, love,
peace, and truth, offering us abundant life!

Jesus, I believe you are the Bread of Life,
broken and given for the life of the world.

Jesus, I believe you are the Light of the
world, who frees us from darkness and an-
swers the deepest questions of our hearts.

Jesus, I believe you are the Good Shepherd,
who laid down his life for us and keeps us
safe, and who calls us to shepherd others.

Jesus, I believe you are the Resurrection, prom-
ising eternal life to all who believe in you.

Jesus, I believe you are the Master who became the servant of all.

Jesus, I believe you are the living and true
Vine who promises plentiful fruit and life
to all the branches who remain united
to you.

Jesus, I believe you are the Way, the Truth,
and the Life of the world, inviting us to
enter into your own relationship with the
Father and be transformed in you.

༄

Following Jesus Way

Jesus invites us not only into communion with himself, but into the loving embrace of the Trinity, to share in his very relationship with the Father and the Spirit. To "remain" in Jesus means to let our entire life be shaped by the absolutely faithful love of a God who pours himself out for the Beloved.

Reflect on the ways God has poured out blessings on you: in your family, in your friendships, in your life of faith, in your vocation. How has God worked in you and through you? in your accomplishments, in your weaknesses? in the past day, week, or month?

In gratitude, pray:

The Call
By George Herbert

Come, my Way, my Truth, my Life:
Such a Way, as gives us breath;
Such a Truth, as ends all strife;
And such a Life, as killeth death.

Come, my Light, my Feast, my Strength:
Such a Light, as shows a feast;
Such a Feast, as mends in length;
Such a Strength, as makes his guest.

Come, my Joy, my Love, my Heart:
Such a Joy, as none can move;
Such a Love, as none can part;
Such a Heart, as joys in love.

Pondering the mystery of Jesus' Eucharistic love for us, we realize that we, too, are called to pour ourselves out in love for God and for those whom God loves. Jesus said, "Whoever keeps my commandments and obeys them—he it is who loves me, while whoever loves me is loved by my Father, and I will love him and reveal myself to him."

Pause to reflect: How is the Lord inviting you to love more deeply, as he loves you?

For the times you have not loved as the Lord would have, pray:

Act of Sorrow

Lord, you have called me "friend" and
  "beloved,"
even though you know I am weak and sinful.
I am deeply sorry for my sins,
for having broken or weakened my communion with you,
and with your beloved ones—each person
  made in your image.
I pray that your loving mercy
will heal what I have hurt,
strengthen what I have weakened,
and transform me
into a more faithful reflection of your love
  upon earth.

*Ask Jesus, the Divine Master, to pour out
his grace upon you in a very special way today, to bring you to the deepest core of your
vocation:*

God's Dream for Me

Adapted from the writings of
Blessed James Alberione

Your dream, O Master, is to lay hold of me,
to change me with your divine life.

Your dream is to purify me, to free me from
my selfishness and my faults.

Your dream is to re-create me, to make me a
new person in your image.

Your dream is to fill me with your charity, to
make me love the Father and all my brothers and sisters just as you do.

Your dream is to bind me to you with the
closest bonds, to bind our hearts together
as one.

Your dream is to make me strong, to impart
to me your divine power, so that I can
overcome evil and be constant in doing
good.

Your dream is to inflame me with an untiring
zeal to spread your kingdom in the world.

Your dream is to possess me in this life and
in the life to come.

O Master, may your dream for me come true.
May I give all to you, freely.

∽

Sharing Jesus' Life

Prayer nurtures our growth in holiness, allowing God to transform us to become more like Jesus. The chaplet below was developed by Blessed James Alberione to nurture Christ's life in us. Use one or each point of the chaplet as a "launching pad" to pray in your own words your desire for Christ to live in you completely—mind, will, and heart.

Chaplet to Jesus, Divine Master, Way, Truth, and Life
By Blessed James Alberione

1. We Adore You, Jesus Truth

Jesus, Divine Master, we adore you as the Word Incarnate sent by the Father to teach us life-giving truths. You are uncreated Truth, the only Master. You alone have words of eternal life. We thank you for having gifted us with the light of reason and faith, and for having called us to the light of glory in heaven. We believe in you and the teachings of the Church, and we pray that your Word may enlighten our minds. Master, show us the treasures of your wisdom; let us know the Father; make us your true disciples. Increase our faith so that we may reach eternal life in heaven.

2. We Adore You, Jesus Way

Jesus, Divine Master, we adore you as the Beloved of the Father, the sole Way to him. We thank you because you showed us how to live a holy life, making yourself our model. We contemplate you throughout your earthly life. You have invited us to follow your example. We want to follow your teachings, treating everyone with love and respect. Draw us to yourself, so that by following in your footsteps and practicing self-sacrifice, we may seek only your will. Increase hope in us and the desire to be similar to you, so that we may rejoice to hear your words, "Come...inherit the kingdom prepared for you from the foundation of the world.... Just as you did it to one of the least of these...you did it to me" (Mt 25:34, 40).

3. Live in Us, Jesus Life

Jesus, Divine Master, we adore you as the only-begotten Son of God, who came on earth to give abundant life to humanity. We thank you because by your death on the cross, you give us life through Baptism and you nourish us in the Eucharist and in the other sacraments. Live in us, O Jesus, with the outpouring of the Holy Spirit, so that we may love you with our whole mind, strength, and heart, and love our neighbor as ourselves for love of you. Increase charity in us, so that one day we may all be united with you in the eternal happiness of heaven.

4. We Adore You Living in the Church

Jesus, Divine Master, we adore you living in the Church, the Mystical Body of Christ, through which you bring us to eternal life. We thank you for having joined us together as members of the Church, in which you continue to be for humanity the Way, the Truth, and the Life. We ask that those who do not believe may receive the gift of faith, that those who are separated may be brought into full communion, and that all people be united in faith, in a common hope, in charity. Assist the Church and its leaders; sustain the People of God. Lord Jesus, our wish is yours: that there be one fold under one Shepherd, so that we may all be together in heaven.

5. May We Radiate You

Jesus, Divine Master, we adore you with the angels who sang the reasons for your Incarnation: glory to God and peace to all people. We thank you for having called us to share in your saving mission. Enkindle in us your flame of love for God and for all humanity. Live in us so that we may radiate you through our prayer, suffering, and work, as well as by word, example, and deed. Send good laborers into your harvest. Come, Master and Lord! Teach and reign, through Mary, Mother, Teacher, and Queen.

As you conclude your hour of adoration, ask Jesus to allow you to faithfully reflect his love to everyone you meet today, and especially to the first person you come across who seems "unlovable."

Mary, Woman of the Eucharist

༄

Theme

To live the Eucharist in our daily life

Introduction

Pope John Paul II said that "Mary is a woman of the Eucharist in her whole life" *(On the Eucharist in Its Relationship to the Church,* no. 53). Through our Baptism, each of us has been deeply associated to the mystery of Jesus' saving life, passion, death, and resurrection, which is memorialized every time we celebrate the Eucharist. Each of us is called, like Mary, to be "women and men of the Eucharist."

Prayer of Adoration

Jesus, present everywhere,
but uniquely here in the Blessed Sacrament
in this gift of your self-giving love,
we adore you
and we ask you to make us men and women
    of the Eucharist.
Immerse us in your Paschal Mystery,
and help us to say "yes"
to your invitation to participate in your life
    and self-offering.

∽

Adoring Jesus Truth

In the wedding at Cana, Mary's heart beats so closely with that of her Son that she anticipates his desire and action. The wedding feast, with its miraculous abundance of flowing wine, prefigures the Eucharistic banquet in which Jesus gives us his own Body and Blood, a sharing in his abundant life. Especially noteworthy is Mary's response of faith when Jesus seems to challenge her.

Reading
John 2:1–11*

On the third day there was a wedding in Cana of Galilee, and Jesus' mother was there. Now Jesus and his disciples had also been invited to the wedding, and when the wine ran out Jesus' mother said to him, "They have no wine." Jesus replied, "What do you want from me, woman? My hour hasn't come yet." His mother said to the servants, "Do whatever he tells you." Now six stone water jars were standing there, in accordance with the Jewish purification rites, each holding twenty to thirty gallons. Jesus said to them, "Fill the water jars with water." And they filled them to the brim. Then he said to them, "Now draw some out and take it to the head steward." So they took it. When the head steward tasted the water which had become wine—and he didn't know where it came from, while the servants who had drawn the water did know—the head steward called the bridegroom and said to him, "Every man first puts out the good wine, then when they're drunk he puts out the lesser wine; *you've* kept the good wine till *now!*" Jesus did this, the first of his signs, at Cana in Galilee and revealed his glory, and his disciples believed in him.

Reflection

Mary's deep faith is clearly expressed in her ability to trust in her divine Son, even when it seems he is indifferent to the situation. She models the kind of faith we need in our own lives, especially when we wonder how God is present in the difficulties we face. Like Mary, we are called to go beyond a belief simply in the physical presence of Jesus in the Eucharist; we are invited to believe in Jesus' loving presence in each of us, in the Church, in our world, in our life situations right now.

When Jesus pours himself out for love of us at each Eucharistic Celebration, he asks us, "Do this in remembrance of me." Jesus invites us to receive the gift of life he shares with us; he also invites us, in turn, to share that same life with others. And this is perhaps the deepest act of faith: to discover how we are called to be the loving presence of Jesus for others.

To give fully of ourselves means self-forgetfulness and self-sacrifice, but only out of love. We can take some time now to reflect on how Jesus might be asking us to participate more fully in the life-giving mystery of his suffering, death, and resurrection.

We offer ourselves to Jesus, to be united with him and to experience his self-giving love more fully:

Jesus Master,
we offer our entire being to you;
we open ourselves to your love
and ask the Holy Spirit to gradually
   transform us.
May our communion with you
develop in us a capacity for love
which empowers us to be sensitive to others,
and strengthened for self-giving and contin-
   ual adaptation.
May this love make us creative, dynamic, and
   deeply committed
to do something for the Lord and for the
   people of our time.

   —Adapted from the *Constitutions of the Daughters of Saint Paul*

∾

Following Jesus Way

Mary's Canticle, the Magnificat, *is a prayer of praise and thanksgiving, recalling the saving works of God, particularly the redemptive Incarnation. Mary's Canticle also reflects a Eucharistic attitude: "Every time the Son of God comes again to us in the 'poverty' of the sacramental signs of bread and wine, the seeds of that new history wherein the mighty are 'put down from their thrones' and 'those of low degree are exalted' takes root in the world"* (On the Eucharist in Its Relationship to the Church, *no. 58). Let us pray the* Magnificat, *found on page 76, in the joyful light of the Eucharist.*

Like no other person, Mary participated in Jesus' self-offering on Calvary, to the point that Jesus asked her to become the Mother of the Church, and of all humanity, as he was dying on the cross: "Behold your mother!" (Jn 19:27)

We can take some time to reflect now on how Jesus is calling us to participate in his Paschal Mystery.

We ask Jesus for forgiveness and mercy for the times and ways that we have been afraid or resisted entering more deeply into the Paschal Mystery:

To Jesus' Gentle Heart
By Blessed James Alberione

Jesus, Divine Master, we thank and praise your most gentle Heart, which led you to give your life for us. Your blood, your wounds, the scourges, the thorns, the cross, your bowed head—all tell our hearts: "No one loves more than he who gives his life for the loved one." The Shepherd died to give life to the sheep. We too want to spend our lives for you. Grant that always, everywhere, and in all things we may seek to know your will in our lives. Inflame our hearts with a deep love for you and for others.

We ask Mary to help us to live a Eucharistic life:

Mary, we entrust our journey to you.
You abandoned yourself into the loving
   hands of God,

trusting God to work powerfully in your life:
"Behold the handmaid of the Lord."
May our faith in the Lord's Incarnation and
   Redemption be as complete as yours.
You adored the Son of God in your womb,
became a "living tabernacle"
in which your Son was adored by Elizabeth.
May our voices, eyes, and lives radiate his
   light.
You were with your Son on Calvary,
uniting yourself with your Son's self-giving
   love.
Help us to discover our place at the foot of
   the cross,
and how we can give of ourselves more fully
   in love to our brothers and sisters.
You shared most wonderfully in the joy of
   Jesus' resurrection;
help us to allow Jesus' promise of new life to
   transform our lives.
May we recognize the many ways your Son
   remains with us now,
and build a communion of love wherever he
   is present:
in the Church, in the Eucharist, in our families, with each person.

May we live fully the joy, awe, and delight
which this Mystery of Love inspires!

—Inspired by Chapter 6 of *On the Eucharist in Its
Relationship to the Church*

∽

Sharing Jesus' Life

*Mary was so closely united to her Son that
his prayer became her prayer. In chapter 17
of John's Gospel, at the Last Supper, Jesus
prays urgently to the Father on our behalf. In
this first Eucharistic prayer, Jesus prays for his
followers, for us, for our union with him, and
for our union with each other. Let us make
this prayer of Jesus our own, asking Mary to
help us unite our hearts to her Son's.*

"Father, the hour has come; glorify your
Son so that the Son may glorify you, since you
have given him authority over all people, to
give eternal life to all whom you have given
him. And this is eternal life, that they may
know you, the only true God, and Jesus Christ
whom you have sent. I glorified you on earth
by finishing the work that you gave me to do.
So now, Father, glorify me in your own pres-

ence with the glory that I had in your presence before the world existed.

"I have made your name known to those whom you gave me from the world. They were yours, and you gave them to me, and they have kept your word. Now they know that everything you have given me is from you; for the words that you gave to me I have given to them, and they have received them and know in truth that I came from you; and they have believed that you sent me. I am asking on their behalf; I am not asking on behalf of the world, but on behalf of those whom you gave me, because they are yours. All mine are yours, and yours are mine; and I have been glorified in them. And now I am no longer in the world, but they are in the world, and I am coming to you. Holy Father, protect them in your name that you have given me, so that they may be one, as we are one. While I was with them, I protected them in your name that you have given me. I guarded them, and not one of them was lost except the one destined to be lost, so that the scripture might be fulfilled. But now I am coming to you, and I speak these things in the world so that they may have my joy made complete in themselves. I have given them your word, and the world has hated them because they do not belong to the world, just as I do not belong to the world. I am not asking you to take them out of the world, but I ask you to protect them from the evil one. They do not belong to the world, just as I do not belong to the world. Sanctify them in the truth; your word is truth. As you have sent me into the world, so I have sent them into the world. And for their sakes I sanctify myself, so that they also may be sanctified in truth.

"I ask not only on behalf of these, but also on behalf of those who will believe in me through their word, that they may all be one. As you, Father, are in me and I am in you, may they also be in us, so that the world may believe that you have sent me. The glory that you have given me I have given them, so that they may be one, as we are one, I in them and you in me, that they may become completely one, so that the world may know that you sent me and have loved them even as you have loved me. Father, I desire that those also, whom you have given me, may be with me where I am, to see my glory, which you have given me because you loved me before the foundation of the world.

"Righteous Father, the world does not know you, but I know you; and these know that you have sent me. I made your name known to them, and I will make it known, so that the love with which you have loved me may be in them, and I in them."

—John 17:1–26

As we prepare to return to our everyday lives, we can decide on one way we can build unity: an activity we can do as a family that will bring family members closer together, or a personal reconciliation with someone who has offended or hurt us.

Hour of Adoration 3

Jesus, Word of Life

∽

Theme

To allow Jesus to bring newness of life into our particular situation

If possible, ahead of time, choose an article from today's newspaper that impressed you, cut it out, and bring it with you to prayer.

Introduction

We may come to this hour of adoration distracted or tired or worried—and that's okay, because God loves us just as we are and wants us to entrust ourselves to him—all that we are, all that we feel, all that we do, all that concerns us. We take a few moments to tell the Lord what weighs heavy on our hearts. This hour is a precious time in which we can focus our attention on God: to be nurtured,

strengthened, called, and lifted up into the
very heart of God.

Prayer of Adoration

My Jesus, Lord,
I come to you thirsty for beauty:
so often I feel betrayed by the ugliness in the
   world around me,
ugliness that I sometimes help to build.
All-Beautiful One, remind me
of the inner beauty of each person created
   and loved by you.

I come to you athirst for truth;
I see so much senseless suffering
and have so many questions I cannot answer.
You who are the Word of Truth,
help me to understand the real meaning
   of my life
so that all I do flows out of a sense
   of purpose,
out of your deepest call to me.

I thirst for wholeness;
our disrespect for one another tears the
   human family apart,

and fractures my heart a piece at a time.
You can heal the wounds that divide us,
if we let you.
Heal my heart, and the division in every
　　human heart.

You who are All~Good,
I am thirsty for your goodness;
I take for granted the abundance you shower
　　on me every day!
Whether I am in the dark or in the light,
let me always remember that you wish to
　　bless me
and fill me with life.
Let me feel your hand holding mine,
　　reminding me
that you are always with me,
encouraging me to share your own goodness
　　with others.

∽

Adoring Jesus Truth

*The Prologue of the Gospel of John is a
contemplative work, slowing us down to pon~
der the amazing reality of the Incarnation:*

the Word of God, the Second Person of the Blessed Trinity, took on our humanity and dwells with us. We need to take our time with this passage. Try noticing which words are repeated in the reading—words that cannot contain the mystery they seek to express— and allow that repetition to become an "entryway" into pondering the mystery and giftedness of our life in Christ.

Reading
John 1:1–18*

In the beginning was the Word,
and the Word was with God,
and the Word was God.
He was in the beginning with God.
All things came to be through him,
and without him nothing came to be.
What came to be through him was life,
and the life was the light of men,
and the light shines in the darkness,
and the darkness did not overcome it.

There was a man sent by God named John. He came as a witness to bear witness concerning the light, so that all might believe through him. He was not the light, but came to bear witness concerning the light. It was the true light that enlightens every man that was coming into the world.

He was in the world, and the world came to
  be through him,
yet the world did not know him.
He came to his own home,
yet his own people did not receive him.

But all who did receive him, to them he gave the power to become sons of God, to those who believe in his name, those who were born, not of blood nor of the will of flesh nor of the will of man, but of God.

And the Word became flesh
and dwelt among us,
and we saw his glory,
glory as of the only begotten of the Father,
full of grace and truth.

John bore witness concerning him and cried out, saying, "This was the one of whom I said, 'The one who's coming after me is above me, because he was before me.' "

For we have all received of his fullness,
and grace upon grace,

for the Torah was given through Moses,
grace and truth came through Jesus Christ.
No one has ever seen God;
the only begotten Son of God,
who is in the bosom of the Father, he has re-
    vealed him.

Reflection

This rich Scripture passage gives us a glimpse of "the big picture": the inner life of the Trinity, our creation in God, the Word of God entering into the world and into our lives. Most of the time, we need reminders of how wonderfully loving our God is; of how God creates us in love and intends us to live in love; of how God surrounds us with the fullness of grace if we only open our hearts to him.

Jesus, the Word made flesh, is our God coming to us, becoming like us, showing us how sacred our humanity is. Jesus is fully human—he ate, worked, slept, played, loved, cried, laughed, belonged to a family, and opened his heart to the larger "family" of humanity. Jesus tangibly shows us what a truly human life is: living in communion with the Father. Jesus is also our Way to God, because he shares with us his own relationship to the Father.

Jesus wants to draw us into his vital relationship with the Father: he offers himself at every Eucharist to the Father on our behalf; he has left us the living Word of the Scriptures so that he can freely speak to our hearts. Jesus is the Word of Life who helps us to enter more deeply into the heart of our loving God, an encounter that can renew us and transform us every day.

Do we feel this abundance of life? We take a few moments now to reflect on how Jesus' becoming fully human has transformed our lives.

In gratitude, we express our faith in the gift of the Incarnation, of Jesus becoming fully human, by praying:

The Angelus

The Angel of the Lord declared unto Mary.
And she conceived of the Holy Spirit.
Hail Mary...

Behold the handmaid of the Lord.
May it be done unto me according to your
  word.
Hail Mary...

And the Word became flesh.
And lived among us.
Hail Mary...

V. *Pray for us, O holy Mother of God.*
R. That we may be made worthy of the
  promises of Christ.

Let us pray. O Lord, it was through the message of an angel that we learned of the Incarnation of your Son, Christ. Pour your grace
into our hearts, and by his passion and cross
bring us to the glory of his resurrection.
Through the same Christ, our Lord. Amen.

Glory to the Father...

❧

Following Jesus Way

The Lord blesses us abundantly every day
on many levels: the gift of life; the gift of family and friends; the ability to walk, think, act,
and love; the special relationship we share

with God through our Baptism and deepen in each of the sacraments we receive. We can take some time now to pray our personal litany of thanksgiving, by calling to mind all the gifts for which we wish to thank God.

In thanksgiving, we can pray the following Canticle from Isaiah, in which God is inviting Israel to partake of and celebrate the abundance that God offers to us.

Come to the Water
Isaiah 55

Everyone who thirsts,
  come to the waters;
and you that have no money,
  come, buy and eat!
Come, buy wine and milk
  without money and without price.
Why do you spend your money for that
  which is not bread,
    and your labor for that which does not
      satisfy?
Listen carefully to me, and eat what is good,
  and delight yourselves in rich food.

Incline your ear, and come to me;
 listen, so that you may live.
I will make with you an everlasting covenant,
 my steadfast, sure love for David.
See, I made him a witness to the peoples,
 a leader and commander for the peoples.
See, you shall call nations that you do not
    know,
 and nations that do not know you shall run
    to you,
because of the LORD your God, the Holy One
    of Israel,
 for he has glorified you.

Seek the LORD while he may be found,
 call upon him while he is near;
let the wicked forsake their way,
 and the unrighteous their thoughts;
let them return to the LORD, that he may have
    mercy on them,
 and to our God, for he will abundantly
    pardon.
For my thoughts are not your thoughts,
 nor are your ways my ways, says the LORD.

For as the heavens are higher than the earth,
  so are my ways higher than your ways
  and my thoughts than your thoughts.

For as the rain and snow come down from
      heaven,
  and do not return there until they have
      watered the earth,
making it bring forth and sprout,
  giving seed to the sower and bread to the
      eater,
so shall my word be that goes out from my
      mouth;
  it shall not return to me empty,
but it shall accomplish that which I purpose,
  and succeed in the thing for which I sent it.

For you shall go out in joy,
  and be led back in peace;
the mountains and the hills before you
  shall burst into song,
  and all the trees of the field shall clap
      their hands.
Instead of the thorn shall come up the
      cypress;
  instead of the brier shall come up the myrtle;

and it shall be to the LORD for a memorial,
   for an everlasting sign that shall not be
      cut off.

We have just reflected on the abundance that Jesus, the Word of Life, brings to us by sharing our humanity. But for most of us, there are areas of our lives which remain in shadow, which seem untouched by the life and joy that Jesus brings. In the Letter to the Romans, Saint Paul says, "All things work together for the good of those who love God, who have been called" (cf. 8:28).

We can take a few moments to reflect on our own lives right now, and bring to Jesus one particular aspect of ourselves or of our life that seems to drain us or drag us down. We ask Jesus to begin to transform this place of struggle, death, uncertainty, or darkness into something life-giving.

We can pray an act of sorrow for our sinfulness, for the times when we have allowed death, not life, to reign in us:

Act of Sorrow

Loving Savior, you suffered, died, and rose to save us. Fill us with joy and newness of life. Forgive us for the times that we have given in to the darkness of sin: for our weakness in doing good, for doubting your love and your promises, for selfishly holding onto your free gifts to us, for being so self-absorbed that we don't even notice the needs of those around us. Let us again "be baptized into your death" so that we may also live your risen life. Make us signs of joy and newness of life for those around us. Amen.

In the Book of the Prophet Isaiah, God promises: "I will give you the treasures of darkness" (45:3). We can take a moment now to entrust our particular situation of darkness to the Lord, expressing our trust that God will fulfill this promise of bringing newness of life out of death.

∽

Sharing Jesus' Life

We can take out the newspaper article we brought with us. (If we didn't bring an article, we can remember a recent news story.) Read it over again here, in Jesus' sacramental presence. What impressed us about the article? Do we somehow identify with someone (or a group of people) in the article? Or does the article impress us because it goes beyond our experience?

Now, we take some time to pray for the people connected with this article, asking Jesus to bring an abundance of life to the people involved. In praying for this person or people, we open our hearts to the needs of the world and share Jesus' life with them in prayer.

Who else do we want to bring into the abundance of Jesus' life? As we pray for the needs of our loved ones and of the world, we ask Jesus that we may share more deeply in his mission of being a life-giver for our world.

In conclusion, we pray again the Prologue of the Gospel of John, this time as a hymn of praise to Jesus, the Word of Life, who allows us to share with him his sonship as God's Beloved.

As we prepare to return to our everyday lives, we can think of one way to be more aware of the abundance we have in Christ, and how we can concretely foster this newness of life in someone else, whether by an encouraging word, a sharing of material goods, or by a witness of our joy in Christ.

❦

Suggested scriptural readings for additional hours of adoration

Theme	Scripture Passages
Beatitudes	Mt 5:1–12; Lk 6:20–26
Church	Mt 16:13–20; Acts 4:23–35; 1 Cor 12:4–31
Conversion	Lk 7:36–50; Lk 19:1–10; 1 Tim 1:12–17
Discernment	Mk 10:17–22; Eph 3:14–20; Gal 5:13–15
Discipleship/ Holiness	Lk 9:23–26; 1 Pt 1:13–21; 2 Tim 1:6–14
Eucharist	Mt 15:32–39; Jn 6; 1 Cor 11:23–27
Faith	Mt 14:22–33; Mk 9:14–29; Jn 20:19–29
Family	Lk 2:41–52; Eph 4:1–16

God's Fidelity	Is 43:1–7; Rom 8:28–39; 2 Tim 2:11–13
Grief	Lk 7:11–17; Jn 11:1–44
Healing	Mk 5:22–43; Rom 7:18–27
Joy	Is 54:1–17; Phil 4:4–9
Love	Jn 15:9–17; 1 Cor 12:29–13:13
Life in Christ	Gal 5:13–26; Eph 1:3–14
Light	Ps 27; Jn 9:1–41
Mission	Jn 20:11–18; 2 Cor 4:7–17
Peace	Ps 122; Jn 14:23–28
Service	Is 42:1–9; Is 49:1–7; Jn 13:1–17; Phil 2:1–11
Trust	Mt 6:25–34; Jn 14:1–3; Phil 4:4–9
Trinity	Mt 3:13–17; Mt 17:1–8
Unity/ Reconciliation	Lk 15:11–31; Jn 15:1–17

Acknowledgments

We would like to thank all those who have given us permission to include material in this book. Every effort has been made to trace and obtain permission from copyright owners. If there are any inadvertent omissions or errors in these acknowledgments, we apologize to those concerned, and will correct the next edition.

For suggestions and providing source material, we gratefully acknowledge:

Mary Emmanuel Alves, FSP
D. Thomas Halpin, FSP
Sharon Anne Legere, FSP
Bernadette Mary Reis, FSP
Virginia Richards, FSP
Patricia Shaules, FSP
Mary Domenica Vitello, FSP
Lawrence Corcoran, SJ
Mary Teresa Curley

Special thanks to Mary Elizabeth Tebo, FSP, for providing the prayers in "Nourishing Our Lives," and to Diane Lynch for her invaluable support and assistance.

Ashwin, Angela, "Christ, Pouring Yourself Out," "Love of Jesus," *Woven into Prayer,* Angela Ashwin, The Canterbury Press, Norwich, England 1999, © Angela Ashwin, 1999.

Bl. Pope John XXIII, "Oh Living Bread!" *Jesus We Adore You: Prayers Before the Blessed Sacrament,* compiled by Paul Thigpen, Servant Publications, Ann Arbor, MI, 2001.

Bl. Teresa of Calcutta, "Love One Another As I Have Loved You," *The Real Presence Through the Ages,* ed. Michael L. Gaudoin-Parker, 1993, published by Alba House, Society of St. Paul, 2187 Victory Blvd., Staten Island, NY 10314-6603. Used with permission.

Compston, Kate, "Thank You, Scandalous God," *Bread of Tomorrow,* ed. Janet Morley, © 1990, Kate Compston. Published by Christian Aid/SPCK, 1992. Used with permission.

Compston, Kate, "Lord Jesus, Rabbi, Teacher," *Encounters, the Prayer Handbook 1988,* © 1987, Kate Compston. Published by United Reformed Church, 1988. Used with permission.

de Cuehlo, Peggy M., "Lord, You Placed Me Here," CCA-Youth, *Your Will be Done,* published September 1984, reprinted October 1986 by Christian Conference of Asia.

Faber, Father, "Sweet Sacrament," © 1953 (Renewed) Lawson-Gould Music Publishers. All

Goodier, Alban, SJ, "Praise of God's Love," *Daily Prayers for the People of God,* ed. Owen O'Sullivan, © 2000, Owen O'Sullivan, published by SPCK, Holy Trinity Church, Marylebone Rd., London, 2001. Used with permission.

Haugen, Marty, "We Remember," © 1980 by GIA Publications, Inc., Chicago, Illinois. All rights reserved. Used with permission.

Houselander, Caryll, "The Host Life," *Wood of the Cradle, Wood of the Cross,* by Caryll Houselander, © 1995, Sophia Institute Press, Manchester, NH 03108. Used with permission.

Lubich, Chiara, "Give Me All the Lonely People," *Christian Living Today: Meditations,* by Chiara Lubich, trans. Julian Stead, OSB, and Jerry Hearne, New City Press, Hyde Park, NY, 1997. Used with permission.

Lubich, Chiara, "The Heart of All Hearts," *A Call to Love—Spiritual Writings, Volume 1: Our Yes to God, the Word of Life, the Eucharist,* by Chiara Lubich, trans. Hugh Moran, New City Press, Hyde Park, NY, 1989. Used with permission.

Mahony, Cardinal Roger, "Eucharist, the Center of Catholic Prayer," *Guide for Sunday Mass: Gather Faithfully Together,* Liturgy Publications, Chicago, IL, 1997. Used with permission.

McIlhagga, Kate, "Beyond Ourselves," *The Green Heart of the Snowdrop*, by Kate McIlhagga, © 2004, Donald McIlhagga. Published by Wild Goose Publications, 4th Floor, Savoy House, 140 Sauchiehall Street, Glasgow, G2 3DH, Scotland. Used with permission.

Metzner, Joan, "Compassion," *Plucking the Strings: A Personal Psalm Journal*, © 1998, Maryknoll Sisters. Published by Twenty-Third Publications, Mystic, CT. Used with permission.

Nouwen, Henri J. M., "We Come with Broken Hearts," "Our Self-Giving God," "Companion of My Soul," *With Burning Hearts: A Meditation on the Eucharistic Life*, by Henri J. M. Nouwen. Published by Orbis Books, Maryknoll, NY, 1994. Used with permission.

Nouwen, Henri J. M., "Deepen My Faith," from *A Cry for Mercy*, by Henri J. M. Nouwen, copyright © 1981 by Henri J. M. Nouwen. Used by permission of Doubleday, a division of Random House, Inc.

Obbard, Elizabeth Ruth, OCD, "I Believe That You Accept Me," *A Retreat with Thérèse of Lisieux: Loving Our Way into Holiness*, by Elizabeth Ruth Obbard, OCD. St. Anthony Messenger Press, Cincinnati, OH, copyright © 1996.

Pope Innocent VI, "Hail, True Body," translated by J. Oxenham. © 1939 (Renewed) Lawson-Gould Music Publishers. All rights reserved. Used by permission. Warner Bros. Publications U.S. Inc., Miami, FL 33014.

Rupp, Joyce, "We Remember the Bread of Life, "Prayer for Awareness," "Blessed Prayer for Healing," excerpted from *Out of the Ordinary,* by Joyce Rupp, © 2000. Used with the permission of the publisher, all rights reserved. Ave Maria Press, P.O. Box 428, Notre Dame, IN, 46556. www.avemaria-press.com.

St. Alphonsus Liguori, "Jesus, Food of Angels," translated by Vaughn, © 1953 (Renewed) Lawson-Gould Music Publishers. All rights reserved. Used by permission. Warner Bros. Publications U.S. Inc., Miami, FL 33014.

St. Alphonsus Liguori, "My Lord Jesus Christ," *The Holy Eucharist,* by St. Alphonsus Liguori, edited and abridged by Charles Dollen, 1994, published by Alba House, Society of St. Paul, 2187 Victory Blvd., Staten Island, NY 10314-6603. Used with permission.

St. Augustine, "Possess Our Hearts," taken from *A Tapestry of Daily Prayer,* compiled by Patricia Newland, © 1990 Charis (Servant Publications). Used with permission of St. Anthony Messenger Press, Cincinnati, OH 45202.

St. Faustina Kowalska, "Chaplet of Divine Mercy," "Immersed in Adoration," "Embrace the Whole World," "Enfold Me in Your Heart," "Hymn of Thanksgiving," *Diary,* St. Maria Faustina Kowalska, *Divine Mercy in My Soul,* © 1987, Congregation of Marians of the Immaculate Conception, Stockbridge, MA 01263. All rights reserved. Used with permission.

St. Hildegard of Bingen, "Repentance and Reunion," *Prayers of Hildegard of Bingen,* ed. Walburga Storch, OSB, © 2003, St. Anthony Messenger Press, Cincinnati, OH 45202. Used with permission.

St. Katharine Drexel, "Abide in Littleness," "To Be a Messenger of His Love," "For Love and Self-Surrender," "A Spiritual Communion," "O Memorial," *Praying with Mother Katharine Drexel,* Drexel Guild, 1987. Archives of the Sisters of the Blessed Sacrament, Bensalem, PA. Used with permission.

St. Pio of Pietrelcina, "Stay with Me, Lord," *The Essential Catholic Handbook of Sacraments,* a Redemptorist Pastoral Publication, 2001. A Redemptorist publication can be used with permission of Liguori Publications, Liguori, MO 63057-9999, (800) 325-9521. No other reproduction of this material is permitted.

St. Thérèse of Lisieux, "Morning Offering," from *The Prayers of St. Thérèse of Lisieux,* translated by Aletheia Kane, OCD, © 1997 by Washington Province of Discalced Carmelites, ICS Publications, 2131 Lincoln Road N.E., Washington, DC 20002-1199 U.S.A. www.iscpublications.org.

St. Thérèse of Lisieux, "To Communicate His Life to You," quoted by Chiara Lubich, *The Eucharist,* by Chiara Lubich, New City Press, Brooklyn, NY, 1977.

St. Thomas Aquinas, "Godhead Here in Hiding," translated by G. M. Hopkins, © 1951 (Renewed) Lawson-Gould Music Publishers. All rights reserved. Used by permission. Warner Bros. Publications U.S. Inc., Miami, FL 33014.

Society of Jesus, "Novena of Grace," *Hearts on Fire: Praying with Jesuits,* ed. Michael Harter, SJ, 1993. Used with permission: © The Institute of Jesuit Sources, St. Louis, MO. All rights reserved.

Stuart, Janet, "Spirit Seeking Light and Beauty," © 1953 (Renewed) Lawson-Gould Music Publishers. All rights reserved. Used by permission. Warner Bros. Publications U.S. Inc., Miami, FL 33014.

Women of Brazil, "Give Us Courage," World Day of Prayer, Women of Brazil (1998). Used with permission of World Day of Prayer International Committee, NY.

Women of Sweden, "For the Troubled of the World," World Day of Prayer, Women of Sweden (1984). Used with permission of World Day of Prayer International Committee, NY.

Pauline
BOOKS & MEDIA

The Daughters of St. Paul operate book and media centers at the following addresses. Visit, call or write the one nearest you today, or find us on the World Wide Web, www.pauline.org

CALIFORNIA

3908 Sepulveda Blvd, Culver City, CA 90230 310-397-8676

5945 Balboa Avenue, San Diego, CA 92111 858-565-9181

46 Geary Street, San Francisco, CA 94108 415-781-5180

FLORIDA

145 S.W. 107th Avenue, Miami, FL 33174 305-559-6715

HAWAII

1143 Bishop Street, Honolulu, HI 96813 808-521-2731

Neighbor Islands call: 866-521-2731

ILLINOIS

172 North Michigan Avenue, Chicago, IL 60601 312-346-4228

LOUISIANA

4403 Veterans Memorial Blvd, Metairie, LA 70006 504-887-7631

MASSACHUSETTS

885 Providence Hwy, Dedham, MA 02026 781-326-5385

MISSOURI

9804 Watson Road, St. Louis, MO 63126 314-965-3512

NEW JERSEY

561 U.S. Route 1, Wick Plaza, Edison, NJ 08817 732-572-1200

NEW YORK

150 East 52nd Street, New York, NY 10022 212-754-1110

78 Fort Place, Staten Island, NY 10301 718-447-5071

PENNSYLVANIA

9171-A Roosevelt Blvd, Philadelphia, PA 19114 215-676-9494

SOUTH CAROLINA

243 King Street, Charleston, SC 29401 843-577-0175

TENNESSEE

4811 Poplar Avenue, Memphis, TN 38117 901-761-2987

TEXAS

114 Main Plaza, San Antonio, TX 78205 210-224-8101

VIRGINIA

1025 King Street, Alexandria, VA 22314 703-549-3806

CANADA

3022 Dufferin Street, Toronto, ON M6B 3T5 416-781-9131

¡También somos su fuente para libros, videos y música en español!